SHADOWS
ON THE
WATER

SHADOWS
ON THE
WATER

THE HAUNTED CANALS AND WATERWAYS OF BRITAIN

ALLAN SCOTT-DAVIES

The History Press

Crick Tunnel, Grand Union Canal.

First published 2010

The History Press
The Mill, Brimscombe Port
Stroud, Gloucestershire, GL5 2QG
www.thehistorypress.co.uk

British Library Cataloguing in Publication Data.
A catalogue record for this book is available from the British Library.

ISBN 978 0 7524 5592 1

Typesetting and origination by The History Press
Printed in Great Britain
Manufacturing managed by Jellyfish Print Solutions Ltd

CONTENTS

ACKNOWLEDGEMENTS

I would like to thank Helen, for proof reading the first draft; Laura, for her search for stories; Kerry Dainty; Richard Smith; everyone at British Waterways, including Neal Owen, Bob Gee, James Clifton, Julie Willetts, Mark Hines, Denis Pike, Terry Drake, Melissa Ezuchukwu; and special thanks to Jenny Histead for all her help publicising the book; Bridget Glynn-Jones (The Wey & Arun Canal Trust); Martin Ludgate; Jenny Black (Waterway Recovery Group); Mike Webb; Sarah Palmer of *Towpath Talk*; John Davies; Colin Hart (BA); Bob Gough (Huddersfield Canal Society); Richard Holland of *Paranormal Magazine*; Dot Moody, her family and Ann Smith of ITV. There are many others I have met along the way who wish to remain anonymous, so thanks go to them, too, for sharing their stories and experiences.

INTRODUCTION

The inland waterways of the mainland United Kingdom have a wealth of history – overcoming challenges of getting from one place to another via tunnels, over aqueducts and through cuttings where shadows lurk. Rivers, lochs, meres and lakes may look romantic in the bright sunlight, but stay until sunset and the shadows slowly creep out of the dark and cold depths of the waters to seek out living souls to take. Over the years I have compiled numerous stories about ghosts and this is a collection of tales from many sites across the land, from mermaids trapped in pools to the Loch Ness monster, from phantom ships and barges full of bodies to helpful giants rising up to carry people across raging torrents of water. There are stories from rivers and canals that will make the hairs on the back of your neck stand up, and others that are simply amusing.

Once I had a list of locations in mind for this book, I set off on my travels to sketch the haunted sites and meet the people who had been in touch with me following a British Waterways press release and articles in *Towpath Talk* and *Paranormal Magazine*. It has been an exciting time, as I was filmed with Kerry Dainty by ITV and interviewed on the radio and via the Internet. There have also been some scary moments such as when I thought I had met the ghost at Badger Dingle in Shropshire … it turned out to be a reveller who just fell over rather than vanished as we walked towards each other through the dingle!

The stories behind the hauntings are often macabre and tragic, usually associated with someone whose life ended too quickly, thus leaving their image imprinted on the screen of time to reappear in certain conditions for viewers to perceive as ghosts. My belief is that we all have the ability to see these images, but as we get older and our parents wean us from our invisible friends we soon forget to 'look'. It has been a great adventure turning up at haunted sites to check details. I have met those who have witnessed the apparitions and sketched the locations, taking photographs too.

So, what is a ghost? Well, there are many theories, and the one I promote from my own research and findings is that a ghost is a video-type image generated at times when all the elements are right for it to appear. Could this be why we tend to see more ghosts at night, the low-light energy images showing up better in the dark? Why do we tend not to see many in daylight – are they still there, but not strong enough to be seen? My theory is that we all have a battery of energy to see us through a full life, from birth to natural death. If we die before our natural time, murdered or the victim of a sudden accident, then we leave a trace image of ourselves powered by the remainder of the battery power that can go on for many more years than if we were alive. Imagine it a little like a projected image through sheets of time, and as time moves on so fades the image.

The Roman soldiers that walk in the cellar of Treasurer's House in York have been getting fainter in image as time passes. We do not typically hear reports of giant mammoth spectres, so time must play a part in erasing their images. There are one or two 'ghosts' that do not fit this theory, and they tend to be the destructive ones who are often linked to suicides or girls developing into young women, plagued with a poltergeist for a short time.

There are more ghosts in Great Britain than in any other part of the world, according to the Ghost Club, and this could well be down to the mix of early invaders from Europe, each bringing traditions and stories to add to those already told here. Whatever the cause, there are many more tales waiting to be discovered and new ghosts making debuts all over the country – so look out for them.

The stories in this book are based on a combination of my own findings and first-hand accounts from people I have met or been in touch with after my appeals for ghost stories related to Britain's waterways. Local variations are taken into account when writing them up, and in this respect various tourist information centres, canal societies and local press contacts have been very helpful. Additional research has been carried out via the Internet and other books, with the parnormal database being used as a point of reference to follow up stories.

If you have any of your own stories about ghosts that inhabit the waterways, be they canals, pools, lakes, lochs, rivers, or any body of inland water, do let me know. May I take this chance to thank you for reading this far, and hope that the rest of the book is of interest to you.

Allan Scott-Davies

CHAPTER ONE

SCOTLAND

BEAULY FIRTH, THE OLD INN

Not only known as a place where smugglers and distillers of illicit whisky would meet, the inn has its share of ghosts too – or so it would seem from the stories put out into the community by the smugglers who gathered there. For many years, people would keep away at night for fear of running into one of the headless coachmen who pounded the narrow lanes to and from the inn. Little did they suspect the ghosts were really smugglers, who used a form of fluorescent paint to make the phantom headless coachmen appear spookier by glowing in the dark.

There is one resident ghost, however, reputedly one of the later landlords who lived, breathed and loved the inn, so as age caught up with him he reluctantly put it up for sale. The night before he was due to move out he suffered a heart attack at the top of the stairs and died. Ever since he returns to visit his beloved tavern, checking the cellar and an old wooden till he used that is now on show, before sitting in his favourite seat, watching the customers enjoy a night at his inn – just as he did in life. But be warned – do not sit in his chair or you may well be pushed out of it!

TARBAT COTTAGE, FEARN

Near Fearn, in the parish of Tarbat, so the ghost story goes, was a muddy pond that once had clear waters washing up against the low bridge from the burn that fed it. Nearby was a cottage with a heather roof, in a style typical for the area. It was here that a grisly murder was committed.

A young pedlar of pots and pans arrived at the empty cottage, enjoyed a small but simple meal, then bedded down for the night. A highwayman who was keen to make a profit attacked him in the middle of the night. He stole the pedlar's goods, chattels and money, before clubbing him to death and throwing his body into the pond. Some time later, the pedlar was seen rising from the lake and walking towards the cottage, as if looking for something – or someone. The locals noticed too that the lake was becoming darker in shade every spring, and began to silt up slowly year on year.

At the water's edge and also in Tarbat Cottage a figure in grey was often seen apparently searching for something. Some sixty years after the murder the sightings faded and the old cottage was bought by a local man who rebuilt it, restoring it to its former glory in preparation for his wife. He lovingly carried his new wife over the threshold on the first night of their honeymoon in their new home. On their third evening together as newlyweds they were preparing for bed, when they heard a great commotion in the kitchen with sounds of banging and thrashing. They watched with horror as their bedroom door opened and the figure of a young man entered the room. The new owner of Tarbat Cottage pulled a poker into his hand from the bedroom fireplace and went toward the intruder, ready to strike. As he did so the intruder spoke, telling them that sixty years ago a highwayman had murdered him, throwing his body into the pond. He informed them that his correct allotted time to die as an old man was fast approaching, and smiled as he proceeded to age before their very eyes, slowly fading into the fabric of the cottage. The next day the skeleton of the young pedlar was found in a newly dug trench where the pond once was. His remains were taken to the nearby churchyard and buried with due ceremony. The ghost of the pedlar has never been seen again.

Tarbat Cottage remained a loving home and a small burn returned to the site of the pond in the following spring, filling with gleaming water that reflected back onto the cottage. Had the man not restored the cottage and moved in, the ghost of the lonely pedlar may still be roaming in search of his killer and goods.

RIVER CONON, HIGHLANDS

Beware if you walk or paddle in the river at Conon Bridge, for it is in the shadows of the bridge that a spirit lurks, appearing as a wave before pulling its victims under water to drown. Dogs have also been known to drown there. The spirit then throws its victim into the air and pushes the lifeless body to shore. The river is also host to the king otter, who, if caught, will grant one wish in return for freedom.

In the shadow of Canon House on the river is a ford. It was here that a servant of Lord Seaforth, on his way home from a party with his two friends, was attacked by the spectre of the river. The servant was crossing the ford on horseback when he emitted a sudden scream and there was frantic neighing, as both man and horse were grabbed and pulled under the water by a large black shape that leapt from the river. The two men watched in horror as their friend's body was thrown to the air before being pulled back into the river. His horse made it to the other side and galloped off home, but despite days of searching, the servant was never found. His ghost appears nearby to warn others away from the ford.

RIVER KYLE, CARBISDALE CASTLE

The castle was built in 1905–1917 for the dowager Duchess of Sunderland, as part settlement after a long legal case over her husband's will, contested by his son. It a safe haven for the King of Norway during the Second World War and in 1945 it became the showpiece of the Scottish Youth Hostel Association. The ghost of a gardener haunts the grounds and attaches itself to girls who are the same age as his lost daughter, who was fifteen years old. He walks along the river bank where his daughter was swept away in a flash flood as she paddled in the shallows. The figure is dressed in a hooded coat, with only part of his face showing.

LOCH ASSYNT

There are a number of stories concerning the area of Loch Assynt, including the sad tale of a pedlar, Murdoch Grant, who was murdered as he travelled around the paths, trading goods and lending money.

It was known that Murdoch carried all his cash on him, as he mistrusted banks, and his home was often broken into. He was last seen alive on the morning of 11 March 1830 as he set off to sell his wares at a wedding in Assynt; a wedding at which he never arrived. A month later, his body was discovered floating in the loch by a courting couple. Murdoch Grant's body was removed from the loch and laid in a coffin. In a strange local custom the residents of Assynt were asked to press their forefinger on the forehead of Murdoch to prove they were not the killer. This is a tradition known as 'touch-proof', as it was believed that a guilty person would bleed from the finger on contact with the corpse.

Only one person refused to do this, saying he was an educated man who did not believe in such poppycock. He was the local schoolmaster, Macleod. Suspicion immediately fell on him, supported by the fact that he was known to be in debt and had a reputation for buying favours of women and living beyond his means. As there was no factual proof, and Macleod claimed his sudden wealth had come from an inheritance, the police had no evidence against him. However, Macleod did not get away with his crime. What he did not count on was Kenneth Frazer, a local man with the gift of second sight.

Frazer walked into the magistrates' court and told an astounded audience of how Macleod had met Murdoch and tried to extend a loan. Murdoch refused and Macleod had hit him on the head then stole the rucksack, taking the money and some of the goods before hiding it in a nearby hollowed out tree. Macleod was arrested for the murder and quickly confessed. He was sentenced to the gallows. Since 1830, each year on 11 March, the sickening noise of lead hitting flesh is heard, followed by a long sigh then running footsteps.

On the shore of the Loch Assynt stands Castle Ardvreck, occupied for nearly one hundred years by an old dowager who liked nothing more than stirring up gossip in the area. One such piece of gossip concerned her daughter-in-law, who the old dowager despised and who had just given birth to a baby boy. The dowager told her son that the baby was not his and that his wife had been having an affair with a woodsman. Enraged, her son rode off to punish his wife for the accused infidelity. Things became so bad that the wife was forced to seek help from her two brothers, and begged them to come and visit her to try and make her husband see sense and realise that the whole story was just a vindictive rumour started by his mother.

The brothers duly arrived, and within a few minutes of meeting the husband a massive row ensued. The younger brother had studied the black arts and, being the strongest of the pair, he forced his sister's husband to the castle where he demanded an audience with the dowager to find the underlying cause of the matter. The brother demanded answers to the questions about his sister's reputation, and as to where the story of her affair had originated.

The dowager refused to say anything, whereupon the brother drew some strange symbols on the floor of the room and shouted out a command towards the loch. At that moment, the waters of the loch boiled up and from them emerged a tall shadow of a man. 'Has she been unfaithful?', the brother asked him. 'No, she is faithful', came the reply. The shadowy man stayed, asking for payment in the form of a human soul. Her son offered the dowager to the shadow man, but she was not accepted. The ghostly apparition then vanished.

The husband returned home full of remorse and ready to beg his wife's forgiveness, only to find his wife in a state of distress: their son had passed away at the same time as the ghost vanished. His wife said she had seen a shadow take the baby boy, saying he was collecting her husband's debt. In the years that followed the crops repeatedly failed and no fish were caught in the loch. At the end of five years there was a massive fire that destroyed the castle in which the dowager perished, carried off to the depths of the loch by the shadow that had been summoned.

It is believed locally that if you see the shadow of the man you will suffer a death in your family within the year.

LOCH MULLARDOCH, HIGHLANDS

Loch Mullardoch is well known for its spectacular walks among the Munro peaks in a remote part of the Highlands. A pair of walkers was descending the peaks when they noticed a small cottage at the edge of Loch Mullardoch that did not appear on their map. Stopping for a break they noticed the cottage seemed to shimmer in the heat of the sun, and they decided to walk towards it to see if it was inhabited as they were looking for a new home in the area. A small dip in the hill meant that they lost sight of the cottage for a short while. When they came over the top of the hill they were surprised to find the cottage had vanished. They asked about the cottage later that evening when they rested their weary limbs in the local inn. To their surprise they were told that, yes, the cottage was well known locally. It had been a lodge for the nearby hunting estate and was just as they had described, but it was now some 30ft below the water of the loch after the water level was raised in the 1950s.

MORAY FORTH, CASTLE STUART, HIGHLANDS

Eight bedrooms in this hotel are named after the clans who lost men when they fought alongside Bonnie Prince Charlie at nearby Culloden in 1745. Perhaps it is the anger felt by these lost men that lives on in the haunted tower of the hotel? After the battle, as the dead and wounded returned home past the castle, many looked up at the tower and saluted it.

Such was the strength of feeling regarding the tower that the Earl of Moray offered a reward to anyone who could stay in it all night to find out what haunted it. A local poacher, Big Angus, took the challenge, and so, after a drink with the Earl, he went upstairs to meet the ghost. The next day he was found in the courtyard, dead, a look of sheer terror on his bloodied face. Also strange was that the window of the tower did not look as if it had been opened – in fact, it could not be opened.

BURN OF LYTH, ACKERGILL TOWER

Ackergill Tower has a long history behind it, that of a feud between the Keith family, who owned the tower, and the Gunn family, who lived across the Burn of Lyth. The two families often raided each other, and on one such raid Helen Gunn was kidnapped and brought back to the tower, where the males of the Keith family drunkenly fought for her while she watched on in horror, surrounded by servants. Helen managed to escape and ran up into the tower room where she prised open a window and leaped out to her death to escape being raped by a Keith male. Her ghost runs up the stairs and is seen exiting the window in the form of a mist moving towards the burn, which she then crosses over on her way home.

RIVER SPEY, BOAT OF GARTEN

On the river bed at Boat of Garten sits an inscribed stone protected by a guardian, a white horse, to make sure that anyone who touches it is cursed.

The legend, which can be traced back to the Middle Ages, goes that a witch would sit on the stone and wait for the village inhabitants to bring her food and drink. The villagers grew tired of her demands and constant moaning. Finally a group of men beat her up and threw her body into the river. Some days later a beautiful white horse appeared standing on the stone as the river rose around it. The villagers worked hard to save it from the waters. As they pulled the horse ashore it turned into the witch, who cursed them all before turning back into the horse and galloping off into the nearby woods. Since then, anyone attempting to sit on the inscribed rock is thrown off, and the white horse appears as if to chase the offender away.

ALLT LAGAN A' BHAINNE STREAM, INVERNESS-SHIRE

The remains of a bridge sit either side of the Allt Lagan a' Bhainne stream, haunted by a ghostly Highlander who looms up out of the mist with two deer hounds by his side, proclaiming, 'that way lies your road', as he points to the broken bridge.

A new footbridge spans the stream these days, so do beware and make sure you do not follow his directions over the ghost bridge and end up in the stream! The ghost is not always seen, but the sense that someone is in the mist pervades the immediate area surrounding the bridge and dogs will often refuse to cross it.

THE LOCH NESS MONSTER

It would not be fair to bring up the Caledonian Canal without mentioning its most famous inhabitant of all – the Loch Ness monster. The Loch Ness monster was first reported in AD 565, in the writings of St Columba, said to have appeared in the deep waters of Loch Ness that are now overlooked by Urqhuart Castle. Nessie, as she is fondly called, has been seen throughout the centuries rising out of the waters of the loch before returning to her deep underwater cave. Many witnesses relate having taken pictures of the ghostly monster swimming in the loch, describing its long neck and distinctive body measuring approximately 40ft long, only to find later that the film is blank and just shows the loch and surrounding landscape.

Some believe Nessie to be the spirit of the loch that appears at times when Scotland needs something to believe in, or is in danger from invading forces. Since 1933 over 3,000 people have reportedly seen the Loch Ness monster, including scientists, police officers, visitors and locals. There is an on-going investigation into Nessie, but like a ghost, she remains a mystery that has many of us intrigued as to what, and who, she really is.

The Loch Ness monster.

ODHAR, CALEDONIAN CANAL

A well-known seer from Scotland, known as Odhar, predicted the opening of the Caledonian Canal. Odhar said that in years to come boats would sail through the hills of Inverness – a prediction that was met with much ridicule at the time. His words were to come true: the great Caledonian Canal opened in 1822 and ships sailed through the hills of Inverness, just as he predicted.

LOCK SEVEN

At lock seven of the Caledonian Canal there have been sightings of an old man carrying a windlass (the winding handle to open and close lock gates) looking down the canal as if waiting for a boat that never appears. This has put off boaters entering the lock for fear that he is waiting for a boat coming in the other direction. It is not until the real lock keeper arrives that the witnesses of the ghostly visitor realise what they have just seen.

LOCH MORAR

During a fishing trip in 1969 two friends, Duncan McDonnel and William Simpson, were rowing on Loch Morar when they hit what they described as a long serpent of 30–40ft in length with three humps and a head a foot wide. The monster became angry due to the collision and retaliated by smashing into the boat with its thick tail. McDonnel shot at the monster with his rifle, causing it to disappear back into the waters of the loch.

The monster has been nicknamed Morag, and over the years she has attracted the attention of the Loch Ness Monster hunters who have visited and tried to capture her image – without results, yet.

LOCH MAREE

In Loch Maree is the spectre of the Muc-sheilch (pronounced Mook Helluch) that has been seen by many anglers and farmers. The Muc-sheilch is described as the monster that moves silently across the water, as a giant eel or snake would do. One man was so excited by the thought of capturing the monster that he part drained the loch and then used quick lime to poison the rest of it. Nothing of the monster was found and the locals ran him out of town for the damage he had inflicted on their loch and fish stocks. That was back in 1850 and the spectre of the monster continues to be seen as a large ripple crossing the loch.

Muc, in Gaelic, means whale, so could the beast be the ghost of a long-gone whale trapped in the loch as the waters receded after the last ice age?

FEARDER BURN, ABERGELDIE, BRAEMAR

Where the Fearder Burn meets the River Dee stands the old mill of Inver, once haunted by a giant black hand. The hand terrorised the mill for hundreds of years and the Davidson family seem to have suffered the longest. One dark and cold night, John Davidson saw the giant hand while he was working in the mill. Engrossed in the work of milling, he looked up from the stones to see the black, sinewy, hairy hand floating above him. He claimed that as he fought the hand, it revealed that it was from a murdered soldier who had had his hands cut off with his own sword before his captors threw him into the River Dee to drown.

After the fight, Davidson was seen digging in the far corner of the courtyard. The hand had indicated that the sword would be found in the close vicinity. John Davidson was rewarded for his effort and unearthed a wrought basket-hilt broad sword that later hung above the fireplace of the mill for many years. The giant hand stopped terrorising the area from that day on, but the figure of a soldier is still seen around the mill and in its grounds.

SPINNING JENNY, RIVER DEE

Along the banks of the River Dee at Ballater is the ghost of a wool spinner, nicknamed Spinning Jenny after the device she is seen using to spin the wool. The story goes that Jenny was washing wool in the River Dee when a sudden downpour high up in the Cairngorms resulted in a flash flood. Jenny drowned, caught by the floodwaters, and her body was found some way down the river. Jenny was still holding a handful of wool and the spinning jenny tied over her shoulder. From that day on, the ghost of Jenny has been seen along the banks of the river, from the place she would have first been swept into the river to the site where her body was discovered. It is said that, should you see her, you should get as far away from the river as you can, as another flash flood is likely to be on its way.

Spinning Jenny, River Dee.

RIVER DEE, ARDOE HOUSE HOTEL, NEAR ABERDEEN

Once a great family home full of fun and joy, Ardoe House was shut up and eventually sold after the daughter of the owner committed suicide when her father forbade her to marry the son of a local laird. Such was her distress, weeping and screaming, that she was locked in a room on the second floor to keep her safe. It was from a window in that room that she fell to her death, having left a reproachful letter for her father. Since then the ghost of a young woman walks the banks of the river and up to the house, now a high-quality hotel.

FIRTH OF TAY, HMS *UNICORN*

HMS *Unicorn* is a fine example of a wooden warship, built in 1824 and moored in Dundee. Staff reports tell of the occasional sighting of a shadowy figure, and the sound of heavy footsteps when the frigate is closed to the public.

FIRTH OF TAY, HMS *DISCOVERY*

The ghost of Charles Bonner is often sensed on board the HMS *Discovery*. Bonner died of injuries in 1901 when he fell from the crow's nest in a storm on the other side of the world. His presence is felt on the section of deck where his life ebbed away whilst the ship's surgeon battled to save his life.

FIRTH OF TAY, TAY BRIDGE DISASTER

During a violent storm on the night of 28 December 1879, the middle section of the bridge collapsed, taking with it a passenger train and all seventy-five passengers. The son-in-law of the designer, Sir Thomas Bouch, was one of the victims of the disaster that was caused by the storm's high winds, with which the design of the bridge could not adequately cope. During the enquiry that followed, engineers found that the columns supporting the thirteen longest spans were weak, leading to the collapse. So great was his distress at the loss of so many lives, Sir Thomas passed away in his sleep less than a year later. To this day, on the anniversary of the disaster the train with carriages is seen glowing red as it travels on the course of the first bridge, the stumps of which remain, before vanishing into the dark waters below.

GLENDHU BURN, BENDERLOCH, OBAN

In the valley of Glendhu Burn roams the ghost of an angry, powerfully built clansman wearing a kilt and carrying a dirk (a Scottish knife), ready for action. Colin Campbell of Glenure was shot on 14 May 1752 after the clans were suppressed, their lands confiscated and the kilt banned.

One witness of this ghostly figure was Sir Hubert Stewart Rankin, the owner of the estate. Whilst walking back to the lodge he saw the figure of Campbell standing in his way, gesturing with his sword towards an invisible foe in front of him. Rankin watched in amazement, for he could see through the figure to the lodge behind it. As he got closer he was able to see the badge of office being worn by the ghost, which helped to identify him. Within yards, Rankin saw the ghost turn towards the lodge and vanish into thin air. He recounted the story to his fellow guests, who all rushed out to seek the ghost for themselves.

BARBRECK, ARGYLLSHIRE

Do not be surprised to find a lonely girl sitting on a large rock in the middle of the River Barbreck, between Ardfern and Ford and near Loch Craignish. She has long red hair with a pale face covered by a hood, and wears a long skirt in an unidentified dark tartan. Whenever she is approached, she turns her head away and appears to melt slowly into the water. Many a young

Ghost on a rock, Barbreck.

man has seen her when under the influence of the local dram and made a valiant attempt to grab hold of the beauty – only to fall into the river for a cold soaking. No one has ever drowned chasing her, as she seems to have more fun getting him, or her, wet and cold.

RIVER ARAY, GLEN SHIRA

It is said that in 1765, a farmer from Glen Aray walked to Glen Shira, accompanied by his son, on a warm summer's day. Having finished business early, they decided to take the walk along the river via Inveraray. At Gairan Bridge they turned north, and as they did so they saw a column of men marching towards them under the command of an officer on a grey horse. The soldiers left the quay, walked along the shore, crossed the river and marched in

Route of phantom army, River Aray.

their direction. The farmer and his son could clearly see the soldiers, with women and children following with their pots and pans. The young son was so convinced that they might abduct him to serve with the army that he jumped over a wall and hid to allow the soldiers to pass.

Hearing nothing, after a few minutes he looked up to see that the soldiers had completely vanished. He rushed to his father's side, who confirmed that he too had witnessed the soldiers. They looked down the track but could find no sign of the mass of men they had just seen. Walking in the direction the soldiers had come from they met a man walking his horse home as the heat was too much for the old gelding. They asked if he had seen the soldiers. He replied that he had not, but reported that he had heard that a column of ghost soldiers had often been seen near the deer park at Gairan Bridge. The father and son looked at each other and a shiver ran down their spines. Later, whilst recounting their tale of the soldier ghosts, they realised that no sound had accompanied the soldiers as they marched on the gravel path.

LOCH FYNE

Whenever the head of the Campbell clan is going to die, a ghostly galleon is said to sail across Loch Fyne to carry the soul of the departed member. The galleon is manned with three crew-members on board and a large seat covered in gold with fine wool blankets adorning it. Some say the galleon continues to sail across the land and into the home of the head of the Campbell clan. It was last seen in 1913.

Inveraray Castle is located on Loch Fyne and has a reputation for a number of ghostly apparitions. The most famous is that of the harpist who walks the corridors of the castle looking through keyholes, a habit for which he was executed after being caught by the Duke's butler spying on the Duke's wife, who was bathing. He had been the harpist for the Duke of Argyll, who was driven from the castle by the Marquis of Montrose in 1644. The Duke left him behind, tied to his harp, with full knowledge that the Marquis would put him to death for being a member of the Duke's household.

The eerie music from a harp is often heard in the library on long summer days. The harpist is joined by the lonely ghost of a young maid, head bowed as she slowly moves through the castle. She is believed to be the ghost of a young maid who was murdered by a Jacobite soldier who took offence to the colour of her hair.

On 10 July 1785, whilst out walking in the grounds with a friend and servant, Sir William Bart and his companions witnessed a ghost battle in the sky. They watched in amazement as a battle was fought between Highland soldiers and French soldiers, with the French forcing back the

Inverary Castle.

Highland soldiers who had to leave behind fallen comrades. Weeks later, word reached the castle that on the day the ghost battle had taken place there was a real battle going on to capture the French-held Ticonderoga fort in Canada, where 300 Highland soldiers had been killed in a bloody battle. The ghost battle has been witnessed on several occasions since in the sky above the castle.

LOCH RANNOCH

There are many tales of times gone by associated with Loch Rannoch. It is here that witches set up a coven to bring down the English as they trespassed into the lands of Scotland. It was also a place where villains hid from the authorities before going back to rob local communities and highways.

Schiehallion Hill, which translates as the Fairy Hill of the Caledonians, has a sinister dog that appears from its shadows and follows walkers down towards the loch and has even been known to try and force people into the icy waters. A white horse has also been witnessed jumping out of the loch and surprising passers-by before galloping across the moor.

As with many of the Scottish waterways and lochs, there have been reported sightings of a monster snake swimming on the surface of the waters of Loch Rannoch.

River Blackadder, Whiteadder, Edrom

On the bank of the River Blackadder, where it meets the River Whiteadder, stood Allanbank, a long-since demolished house that was haunted by a ghost known as Pearlin Jean who is believed to have died in 1789. This story is one of cold-hearted betrayal and murder. Whilst on a trip to France, Robert Stuart met a nun called Jean with whom he fell head over heels in love, and the feeling was mutual. Robert Stuart persuaded her to leave the convent and marry him on their return to Scotland. For a month, they enjoyed each other's company so much so that she finally succumbed to his charms and they made love. Robert Stuart thereupon had a change of heart, and decided she was not the one for him after all. As she lay in bed dreaming of her life in Scotland, Stuart left in his carriage, not even leaving a note by way of an explanation. She waited and waited for word from him, until she overheard the servants talking excitedly of the wedding they had been asked to attend in Scotland.

Jean was so upset by the news that she told the staff of the betrayal and persuaded them to take her with them to Allanbank. She arrived in time to see Robert Stuart driving off with his new fiancée. She ran after them and caught up, stopping the coach and four horses by jumping in front of it. Stuart was said to have gone white with shock when he realised it was Jean, who started to scream at him to get out and explain himself. Jean had positioned herself above the front wheel when the cowardly Stuart told his driver to carry on. As the carriage moved forward, Jean's dress caught in the spokes of the wheel and she was dragged under and crushed to death. No one in the carriage looked back as Jean's life ebbed away on the drive. Her body was buried in the local churchyard, where she was only known to the few servants from Paris who were instantly dismissed for bringing her to Stuart's home.

Stuart was soon married to his new love. Returning home one day from a late meeting, he was shocked to see Jean sitting on top of the coach-house arch. She was dressed in the same long white dress in which she was murdered,

River Blackadder, Scotland.

with blood washing down her face and over her chest. Jean continued to haunt Allanbank, and it was only when a portrait of her was placed between those of Robert Stuart and his wife that the haunting stopped.

The Stuarts left in 1790, letting the house to a family who had no idea about the ghost of Allanbank. Two of their children woke to the sound of someone in a long dress swishing across the floor and the sound of pained breathing. This happened on many occasions, with sightings of Jean in the corridors and even in the orchard. Here Jean spooked a man who had arranged to meet one of the maids at midnight. It was a full moon and the air was still. As he walked across the orchard he saw a woman standing under a tree. He crept up to her thinking it was the maid, making a grab for her waist, and was astonished to find he was hugging the tree trunk. Looking around he once again saw the woman he took to be the maid. As he approached, Jean vanished. The midnight antics were all too much for him and he ran off into the night without keeping his liaison with the maid – whom he later married once the story of why he stood her up was revealed.

Allanbank was finally demolished, but despite this Jean's ghost has subsequently been seen on the site of the house and along the driveway, much to the relief of the local people who have come to love her.

POWSAIL BURN, DRUMELZIER

By the side of the burn that runs through the village of Drumelzier and close to the churchyard lies the grave of Merlin, King Arthur's wizard and guide. Being the son of a Welsh maiden and a demon, Merlin was heading for a path of self-destruction, driven by the evil use of his powers. He was

Merlin.

saved by baptism, yet retained his father's gift of magic throughout his life, turning it to good use to protect his King and country. Merlin was seen to stand by his grave as the burn overflowed, swamping his resting place before pouring into the River Tweed.

At the same time, the prophecy of Thomas the Rymer came true. He wrote that:

> When the Tweed and the Powsail meet at Merlin's grave,
> England and Scotland shall one monarch have.

On the day of the flood, Queen Elizabeth I died and James VI of Scotland became James I of England.

THE FALKIRK WHEEL, FALKIRK

As an icon of modern engineering, the Falkirk Wheel stands proudly between the Forth & Clyde Canal and the Union Canal. When work was underway, the builders reported seeing a Roman centurion walking around the site, most frequently on the towpath of the Union Canal. It is believed that he is one of a number of soldiers who patrolled this area from a nearby Roman fort.

The Falkirk Wheel.

Another ghost seen regularly by walkers along the towpath of the Union Canal near the Falkirk Wheel is that of a man's bedraggled shuffling figure. One couple felt strongly that the ghostly figure was trying to communicate with them and employed a medium to see if they could make contact with him. They apparently discovered that he had run up debts when he came home from the First World War, and with no livelihood had no way of paying them off. He had fled to the area, seeking refuge in the canal tunnel and nearby woods where he managed to eek out a survival. Unfortunately for the man he was informed upon, and it was not long before a Glasgow gang caught up with him to settle the outstanding debts. Penniless and with nothing to give the would-be attackers, his throat was slit and his body thrown into the canal. His body lay undiscovered for many weeks. Since that fateful day he has haunted the towpath, seeking out someone to whom he could tell his woeful tale.

RIVER CLYDE, DALMARNOCK ROAD BRIDGE, GLASGOW

One of eight bridges in the city, this bridge has been used many times by people committing suicide. The ghost of one suicide has been seen on numerous occasions, walking towards the centre of the bridge before stepping up onto the rail and jumping into the sea below. He is described by one witness, a tax inspector, as a young man in his thirties dressed in a three-quarter-length navy coat, black trousers and with a crew-cut hairstyle. The witness saw the man standing by the bridge rails looking towards the Clyde, which made him think he was about to jump. He shouted to the man to stop and rushed towards him. As he got within grabbing distance the young man jumped, yet, as the witness looked over the rail expecting to see him falling to the river, he saw nothing. He was so convinced he had seen a suicide attempt he reported it to the police, who already had the same description from many others. To this day the ghost of the man is seen – often during the day – jumping off the bridge.

BOTHLIN BURN, BEDLAY CASTLE, CRYSTON, GLASGOW

The ghost of the Bishop of Glasgow is said to haunt the castle following his mysterious death in the castle lake after an altercation with a spirit he wanted to send to the light. The hooded figure of a rotund man sometimes touches women on the face before moving off with heavy footsteps through the hall.

The mausoleum of the Campbell family is haunted by a number of shadowy ghosts that even followed the structure when it was moved to a nearby graveyard for safekeeping. The other ghost at the castle appears at the rear gate, where a coach and horses is heard but never seen, before the figure of a young girl steps out into the path of the invisible coach: there is a scream and then silence.

RIVER ESK, EDINBURGH

Dalhousie Castle is now a hotel standing in grounds overlooking the River Esk. In the sixteenth century, the beautiful Lady Catherine of the neighbouring estate embarked upon an affair with the owner of the castle. The affair lasted for years, much to the discomfort of the owner's wife, Eleanor, who was much older than Catherine. After a prolonged absence with his mistress in Edinburgh, her husband returned home with the intention of breaking his marriage to Eleanor in favour of Catherine. A day later, Catherine came to the castle and was met by Eleanor offering her a gift for her marriage, pretending to give Catherine her blessing. Catherine followed her to a tower room where Eleanor opened a large trunk, containing an elegant dress. 'Try it on,' said Eleanor as she pointed to a side door. As Catherine tried on the dress, Eleanor locked her in the room.

Days later a search party was organised to find Catherine, who had not returned from her walk to meet her lover and husband to be. No trace was ever found of Catherine and Eleanor went to her grave with her secret, watching her unfaithful husband die of a broken heart. Many years later, Catherine's skeleton was found in the locked attic room. Her body was buried in the churchyard, yet her ghost is still seen in the castle and down at the river where she meets an older man who takes her hand as they walk together.

RIVER ESK, LASSWADE

A mile up the River Esk is De Quincey Cottage, a house that is haunted – in a friendly way – by the ghost of Thomas De Quincey, who loved nothing more than to take long midnight walks along the river bank. He always carried a large hurricane lamp to light his way and has been seen ever since his death in 1859 walking the river bank at night. Night fishermen report seeing Thomas De Quincey's ghostly light and believe that if the light appears near to a rod the fisherman is bound to catch a large fish that night!

RIVER NORTH ESK, WOODHOUSELEE CASTLE

Lady Bothwell.

At the site of Woodhouselee Castle, you can witness the tragedy of Lady Bothwell, who resided there in 1580 when it was attacked while her husband was away on business. The attackers seized the castle and taunted Lady Bothwell, before stripping her and her small baby of their clothes and throwing them out into the bitter cold night. Her husband, upon his return, commanded his soldiers to remove the now drunken men to a guarded room whilst he searched for his beloved wife and child. He followed the sound of sobbing to the river bank and found his wife naked, blue with cold, madly running with their dead child clutched to her breast. His rage knew no bounds and he slaughtered the invaders of his castle with blows from his mighty sword. Within the week, Lady Bothwell also died. Her ghost began to haunt the river bank, constantly seeking to comfort her dying child. On the site of the castle, the shadows of a group of men appear before fading into the night.

GLADHOUSE RESERVOIR

Before the dam was built and the valley flooded, there was a farmhouse known as Hoolet House, in which a wealthy – but grumpy – middle-aged farmer lived. For many years there was no laughter from the house, and at night light from just one solitary candle shone. That was until the farmer returned home following a visit to Falkirk with a young bride. After that, Hoolet House was a different place. There was laughter and light, and people began to visit. As the years passed, the farmer returned to his old miserly ways. All but one of the servants, a young Irishman, left the house, saying the farmer had become irascible. One day the farmer went to market, little knowing that his wife and the Irishman were planning to run away together. Upon his return he claimed to have discovered they had run away with all his money, £200 or more. He organised a search party, but the couple were never found.

As the months went by people claimed to see the couple around the house, but upon approach they would disappear into the night. At the same time, the animals on the farm began to die of a mystery illness and the farmer had to bury them, employing men to help him when his horse died. The farmer became agitated when they started to dig near a large tree. Too late – a hand was found, and then the mangled remains of the farmer's wife and the Irishman were discovered. The farmer turned on his heels and, as if on a pre-planned escape, rode off with his money and some goods, never to be seen alive again.

After some time of absence, the farm was divided amongst the nearby farmers and the house fell into ruin. No one could put up with the ghosts as they played out the gruesome scene of a double murder, the image of the ferocious farmer slashing away at the flesh of the cowering couple with a billhook, and his anguished screams when he realised what he had done. On moonlit nights, it is said the screams of the victims and the farmer can be heard coming from the depths of the reservoir.

Firth of Clyde, Culzean Castle

Built for the Kennedy clan, Culzean Castle had a remodel by Robert Adam in the eighteenth century. The ghost of a lone piper is heard whenever a member of the Kennedy clan is to be married and when there is a ferocious storm heading towards the castle. A woman dressed in a long ballgown has also been seen, yet there is no evidence to explain who she might have been.

The Kelpie

The Kelpie is a treacherous water devil who appears around the rivers and lochs of Scotland. One famous Kelpie appears along the Caledonian Canal where it enters Loch Locky. The story goes that many a weary traveller has stopped to rest and drink water from the loch. After a few minutes, they report noticing a handsome horse a few yards from where they are sitting. Approaching, they see that the horse is riderless with no sign of an owner, and often attempt to mount the horse to bring it under control. The horse appears to accept its new rider and trots off gently, before turning into a raging gallop and leaping into the cold waters of the loch, whose icy depths claim its victim. Some visitors report seeing a glow travelling deep in the loch, and believe it to be one of the many souls claimed by the Kelpie trying to escape their watery grave.

The Shellycoat

Another Scottish water spirit – or ghost – is the Shellycoat, so named as he is dressed from head to foot in shells from the river bed that make a distinctive rattling whenever he moves. The Shellycoat appears to be an eccentric man who likes to give helpful directions. Be warned though, his motive is mischievous and his directions always incorrect. The Shellycoat watches with glee as the innocent walker finds themselves lost in the nearby glens and gullies.

CHAPTER TWO

NORTHERN IRELAND

BALLYGALLY CASTLE, ANTRIM

Ballygally Castle is reputedly one of the most haunted places in Northern Ireland, where at times there are more ghosts than guests staying in the hotel. It is also has some spectacular views out to the sea and surrounding land. The most frequently seen – and heard – ghost is that of Lady Isobel Shaw, who was unable to conceive a male heir and died in 1635. When she gave birth to a girl her husband was so infuriated that he forced her into the attic room with her child as punishment. As she starved to death on the orders of her husband, a servant was caught taking food and water to her. The servant was taken outside the castle by Lady Isobel's husband and the estate manager, stripped naked and beaten to death, her small broken body thrown into the sea.

From her high vantage point in the tower, Lady Isobel watched the wrath of her husband as he punished the maid and, fearing for her own life, opened the window and jumped to her death while clutching her daughter. Since then, she walks the castle, its meadows and the nearby stream with her child and sometimes with a smiling maid holding the child's hand.

The other resident ghost at the castle is that of Madam Nixon, who lived the last days of her life in a large suite of the hotel in the nineteenth century. She walks along the corridors in a beautiful silk dress, swishing as she walks.

HEADLESS COACHMAN, RIVER FOYLE, DERRY

In 1865 over the River Foyle there was an old wooden bridge that linked the Waterside to the Derry side, on which a local man once had a terrifying experience. On a winter evening he was crossing the bridge towards Derry where there was a wooden tollhouse when a coach and four horses drove through it towards him at speed. No matter which way he moved, the coachman seemed determined to run the man down. Fearing for his life as the thundering noise of hooves and carriage wheels came closer, he jumped up onto the guard rail and watched with horror as the headless coachman drove past and smashed through the rail into the river at the Waterside end amidst the noise of thrashing in the water and screams of distressed horses. As he watched where the coach smashed through the guard rail, a mist covered the damage and started to move towards him.

He was so shaken when he rushed into his local inn that at first no one recognised him, as he had lost weight and his black hair had gone white. Some years later, when the demolition of the bridge was taking place to make way for a new one, the gang taking it down saw a black swirling mass cross the remains of the bridge from the Derry end. They watched in disbelief as the coach went crashing into the river towards the Waterside end, with fearful screams of horses and people followed by complete silence. There have been few sightings since, yet the noise of a coach and four horses racing over a wooden bridge before crashing into the river is still heard.

THE WORKHOUSE, RIVER FOYLE, DERRY

A blue guardian who paces the corridors and rooms, remonstrating with herself over her foul – yet accidental – deed, haunts the old workhouse in Glendermott Street on Waterside. She was a middle-aged woman in charge of the children in the workhouse and responsible for punishing the naughty ones. This was the part of her job she hated, but after a strict warning and the risk of losing her post for being too lenient with the children, she had to increase her measures. The worse punishment she administered was to lock a boy or girl in a cupboard at the top of the building until they had learnt their lesson.

On one occasion, a brother and sister caught trying to run away were placed in the cupboard with bread and water for the night. As she carried out her rounds before lock-up, the guardian received a message from her sister's husband that she had taken ill and he needed help to nurse her back to health. Without a second thought she went off to aid her sister, who lived some miles away. Preoccupied with the nursing and cooking for her sister's family, she completely forgot about the children in the attic cupboard. That was until she was returning to the workhouse in a coach, two weeks later, when she remembered in a flash. Panicked, she urged the coach driver to go faster.

On arrival, she rushed up the stairs to the cupboard to find it still closed. Fearing the worst she opened the doors to find the brother and sister hugging each other, both dead. She screamed and wept, and such was her guilt that she could not be consoled and she passed away in her sleep weeks later. After her death she became the friend of lonely children in the home, helping them from the other side. Seen as a glowing blue spirit, and joined by the ghosts of the brother and sister who hold her hands, they walk together through the building, all smiles. The building was turned into a hospital years later, where one nurse was taken ill and needed an operation. Later that night she woke up cold to see a figure, dressed in white with a blue light around her, place a blanket on her bed before walking through a wall.

Another ghostly happening in the building occurred in a small flat occupied by Matron Edwards, who lived on one of the top floors. One night she awoke to the noise of the taps of the basin gushing out water with such force that it flowed over the bowl and on to the floor. No matter how hard she tried to turn them off, the taps continued to run. She fled the flat and never returned. After being calmed down by the caretaker and a colleague she told them what had happened. The caretaker ran up the stairs to stop the flow of water. In the flat all was calm. A light shone on the sink, yet it was perfectly dry – no sign of a flood.

The workhouse is now a museum and library of great standing. During the redevelopment, a large paupers' grave was discovered in the old yard and the remains given a Christian burial.

GHOST OF FANNY WYLIE'S BRIDGE, DERRY

On the outskirts of Derry lies the village of Ballyarnet, where there is a small bridge crossing a deep stream that a strange little ghost haunts. Near the bridge is a ruined cottage alongside a number of ivy-covered trees. The area has a feeling of loss, even in the daylight, and in the 1950s and '60s people avoided the bridge unless they were in pairs or groups, with the last recorded sighting of the ghost in 1962. A tiny evil-looking man appeared to two women crossing the bridge, waving his hands and shouting before vanishing into the dark followed by a blood-curdling laugh that pierced the cold night air. Some have claimed that they saw the little man jump as high as the top of the trees before appearing in front of them. Whilst he has not been seen in recent years, footsteps have been heard by walkers when no one was around. Needless to say, they do not linger there long.

The ghost at Fanny Wylie's Bridge.

DOCKLANDS, BELFAST

The local company, Direct Wine Shipments, of 5–7 Corporation Square, Belfast, boasts a spirit that is not in a bottle but instead wanders the old warehouse, knocking bottles over and pinging glasses. Is this the restless ghost of one of the many sailors who fell into the dock and drowned after being attacked for their pay when on shore leave?

POOKA

A Pooka is the most feared of the night-time creatures who roam Ireland, often appearing in the pits of water closets from where they emerge into the night to start their reign of terror. They have the head of a man and the body of a goat, horse or dog, and can fly for short distances. When people started to have water closets inside the home, many put heavy weights on the lavatory seat to stop the Pooka from entering the house. They run in packs and are ill-tempered, so when they find a victim they inflict as much harm as possible in a short time before moving on. Any accident that befalls people – children who die, crops that fail and newborn babies who go missing – is blamed on the Pooka, who enjoy hunting for their victims on moonlit nights. As they live in the smelly cesspits of the country, their wretched smell reaches the victim long before the Pooka attacks, so be warned if you are out on a moonlit night and the smell of a cesspit drifts towards you – run!

SION MILLS, RIVER MOURNE, COUNTY TYRONE

Along the river bank of the River Mourne, near the railway bridge, the ghost of a suicide victim is seen falling from the bridge into the river without a noise, the body bobbing up to the surface of the river before vanishing below it.

The ghost of a man and a big black dog have been seen on the bridge at the spot where they were killed by a train that struck them from behind as they took the short cut at the river. Just before these sightings, witnesses have reportedly heard chains rattling.

Close by a white figure has been seen rising from the river and drifting off across the fields towards the village green, where cricket is played. The games are watched by another ghost, that of a keen cricketer who one night, after winning a game, met a banshee on his way home. The experience upset him so much he killed himself on the nearby road, where it is said he can be seen hanging from a tree.

CHAPTER THREE

NORTH ENGLAND

RIVER COQUET, WARKWORTH, NORTHUMBERLAND

A small hermitage on the banks of the River Coquet is dedicated to Isabel and the brother of Sir Bertram with the words, 'My tears have been my meat night and day'.

The story behind this began when Sir Bertram joined Earl Percy to fight Earl Douglas in a fierce battle that left Sir Bertram badly wounded from a blow to his head. As he lay at death's door in Wark Castle he asked for his love, Isabel, to be by his side. To his dismay, she never arrived. When he felt well enough and able to make the journey, he went with his brother to visit her at her home. They discovered that Isabel and her maid had left for Wark Castle immediately on receiving the message to attend Sir Betram as he lay wounded.

The route between the two locations was known as a kidnapper's black-spot. Fearing for her safety, Sir Bertram began to search for his lost love. Eventually he met a monk on the road who told of a beautiful princess held captive in a tower in the Lowlands. Sir Bertram made for the tower, but could not gain access. He took refuge in a cave close by to watch the tower. He was rewarded when, at last, he saw his beloved Isabel framed at a window, so he knew that she was safe and well.

As he set about planning her escape, a tall figure in Highland costume rode beneath the window and threw up a rope to Isabel, who sat waiting in the window. While she climbed down the rope to the mystery Highland man, Sir Bertram crept up behind the costumed figure, and raising his sword he shouted for the man to leave his lady alone before striking him. The man fell to the ground and lay at Sir Betram's mercy. Isabel, having made it to the ground and realising that the attacker was Sir Bertram, jumped between him and the man shouting, 'This is your brother!'

Her words came too late. Sir Bertram was in mid-swing and his heavy broad sword sliced through both Isabel and his brother, killing them instantly. In his remorse, Sir Bertram gave all his land to the poor and built the hermitage, consisting of a tiny chapel, a dormitory and a cell, where he lived and died a broken and lonely man.

Abbey ghosts, Dumfries and Galloway.

RIVER TYNE, SOUTH SHIELDS

Jack the Hammer is a tall sombre figure of a man dressed in a fisherman-style smock and cap carrying a large gleaming hammer. He is seen walking along the river bank of the River Tyne, heading toward the sea. In folklore, when a fisherman dies at sea he is said to attend his home and knock three times to warn those inside of the coming news. Jack the Hammer also watches funeral processions for fallen fishermen.

RIVER NORTH TYNE

On the bank of the River North Tyne stands the proud Haughton Castle, home to the ghost of Archie Armstrong. The area was constantly being raided by the local Scottish clans, and a warden was appointed by the King to keep the trouble under control. Unfortunately, the warden, Lord Dacre of Gilsland, was less than honourable, and was known to be open to bribery. He regularly turned a blind eye to the goings-on of one gang of thieves whose chief was Archie Armstrong.

Lord Haughton was an honest man, who the local farmers turned to for help to quell the trouble and relied on to go to the King on their behalf. Before he left for York for an important meeting with the King's chief minister, Lord Cardinal Wolsey, Armstrong was captured cattle rustling and locked in the dungeon of Haughton to await his fate. Lord Haughton arrived in York and, to his horror, discovered he still had the keys to the dungeon in his jacket pocket. So upset was he that he immediately turned around and headed for home. He had left no instructions for the servants and feared for Archie Armstrong's well-being. He rode so fast that his horse died under him and at Durham he had to borrow another horse to reach Haughton a day later. His servants informed him they had heard Armstrong shouting, then screaming, and confirmed that it was all quiet now. Opening the dungeon door he found Armstrong dead, his face contorted with pain and flesh from his arms missing.

A week later, the ghost of Archie Armstrong appeared in the bedroom of Lord Haughton, screaming in pain, continuing to reappear until the rector of Simonburn exorcised the ghost using a black-lettered bible. The ghost was finally laid to rest. Peace lasted until one day the bible was taken to London for restoration, when the ghost of Archie Armstrong awoke and his terrible cries could be heard once more in the dungeon. As soon as the bible was back the screams went quiet. Nevertheless, the ghost of Archie Armstrong is often seen in the castle and along the river bank.

RIVER TEES, CAULDRON SNOUT WATERFALL

High up on Dufton Fell is the spectacular waterfall known as the Cauldron Snout. It is home to the sad ghost of a young woman, who sits to the side of the raging torrents singing. The daughter of a local farmer, it was during the reign of Queen Victoria that she fell in love with a miner who had been working nearby. When he left without her, she became so distraught with the pain of heartbreak that she threw herself off the rocks at the top of the waterfall and drowned. Two days later, her battered body was found near the spot where she is now said to sing.

Cauldron Snout Waterfall.

RIVER TEES, LOST SOULS

Around the area of Darlington, where the River Tees flows, can be found a series of deep pools of water known locally as the Hell's Kettles. They are caused by the soft rock being washed away, leaving the harder rock in the forms of basins. Within these basins, it is said, are the lost souls of all who have perished in the river from its source to the sea. On clear moonlit nights they become visible at the bottom of the pools – but be warned, if they see you, you could be the next to join them, as the Devil visits to trap lost souls and imprison them in the Hell's Kettles.

RIVER WEAR, COATHAM MUNDEVILLE

The ghost of a nun has been seen in a room of Hallgarth Manor where, during restorations, a body – presumably hers – was found with a small cross close by. She is believed to have been caught having an affair with a monk who was billeted at the hostelry on the site of the present sixteenth-century manor. Punishment for such acts was to be bricked up in a cell alive. The ghost of the nun walks down to the river, where she would have met her lover in happier times on the bank close to Finchale Abbey. Soft sobbing is sometimes heard in the room, followed by the smell of rose water, and taps turn themselves on and off at night.

RIVER GRETA

Along the banks of the River Greta in Durham walks the ghost of the wife of Thomas Rokeby, who owned Mortham Tower and ruled the area during the reign of Henry VII. He was insanely jealous, and after seeing his wife talking to a footman he became so convinced she was having an affair that he cut off her head and threw her body into the River Greta. The headless ghost is seen draped in fine silks the colour of the rainbow. Records show that an eighteenth-century parson met the ghost under the bridge over the River Greta near the tower and had a conversation with her in Latin. Not bad for a headless ghost!

River Greta.

SOLWAY FIRTH, SKINBURNESS

Over the years, couples eloping to get married at Gretna Green have arrived at Skinburness seeking a ferryman who would take them across the Solway Firth. The area is remote and couples often found that they had time on their hands, sometimes even days, waiting for the next ferry to land. It was on one summer's day in the late 1700s when a couple stepped onto the boat of a ferryman, and in the calm of the waters were rowed across to Newbie. Mid-journey, however, their boat was overturned by a freak storm that raged for some minutes from the sea up the Firth towards Carlisle. All three were drowned and their bodies washed up on the shore of Moricambe Bay. To this day, when the wind gets up their screams and cries for help are heard coming from the Firth, and a small rowboat with three cowering figures can be seen vanishing below the waves.

THIRLMERE

In 1894, the whole valley that became Thirlmere was flooded. A house at the bottom of the valley was known locally as the meeting place for all the ghosts of the Lake District, who congregated there on Halloween. It is believed that the ghosts still gather there, as on certain days before and after Halloween the waters of Thirlmere are said to boil up. At the northern end of Thirlmere is an outcrop called Castle Rock that is a popular place for climbers. It is here apparently that the ghosts, not wanting to meet under-water, convene and, for fun, flick at the climbers or even try to push them off the cliffs to meet their death on the rocks below.

RIVER ESK, MUNCASTER CASTLE

In the tapestry room of the castle, two children are heard crying in great pain before being struck silent following a loud crashing noise. A white lady who walks along the road to the castle and along the river bank – and sometimes in the grand hall too – joins them. Their companion is a fool or jester who leaps about the ground-floor rooms, entertaining an invisible audience. The ghost of Mary Bragg, a young woman murdered in the 1800s on the driveway, runs towards cars travelling along it at night, trying to get the attention of the occupants before melting into the darkness.

BUTTERMERE, THE FISH HOTEL, LAKE DISTRICT

The sad ghost of a young woman who was taken advantage of by a rogue haunts the Fish Hotel and surrounding area of Buttermere. She was the fifteen-year-old daughter of the landlord, Mr Robinson, whose beauty was legendary in the 1790s. Many a suitor had tried to woo her, but to no avail. Writers visiting the area mentioned her stunning looks in reports for national newspapers or guides to the area. When a tall dark stranger named Colonel Alexander Hope arrived at the inn, the young woman, Mary, fell in love with him completely. The man lavished gifts upon her from London and Paris, attended to her as if she were a queen, and then asked for her hand in marriage. Her father agreed, believing that the man was wealthy and of good standing.

The story of the wedding reached London, where it featured in the newspapers of the day. A journalist, keen to follow up the story and get background information on the couple, started to dig around to find out more information about the colonel. Little did he know his findings would be the ruin of the young woman. The colonel was not who he claimed to be. In fact he was already married to a women with children, and his family had been abandoned at a workhouse in London. His real name was John Hatfield, an undischarged bankrupt. When the news reached Mary and her family, John fled into the hills, but was captured and later executed in London for the crimes of bigamy and false pretences. Mary was so broken by the experience that she passed away in her room at the inn, where her ghost is seen standing on the stairs, and also by Buttermere, sitting on a rock.

LAKE WINDERMERE

At Wray Castle in the Lake District, a young cadet was helping with maintenance during his summer holidays. He was standing on a tower scaffold at the top of the main stairs and painting the walls when his balance shifted and the scaffolding surged forward. He felt an invisible hand pushing him and forcing him to grab the handrail. Looking down he noticed damp patches appear on the bottom step. Once more, an invisible hand rocked the tower. Terrified, he descended the scaffolding at lightning speed.

Further down the lake, where the car ferry operates, and before the waters of the Cunsey Beck meet, is an area of the lake that many people fear. In 1635, a bride, groom and forty-three of their family and friends drowned as the makeshift ferry that they were travelling on sank to the bottom of the lake in a tragic accident. At night, the screams and frantic splashing of the lost souls can be heard echoing across Lake Windermere.

At the High Wray landing site there has been seen the shadowy image of the body of Thomas Lancaster, encased in a gibbet. He was convicted in 1671 of poisoning his wife and six of her family. Thomas Lancaster had an accomplice to his murders, a young servant who he also killed. The murders took place in Threlkeld, near Keswick, and Lancaster was executed in the place where he was born, as was the tradition of the day. Many a ferryman has heard him call out for a passage on the row boats used to ferry people and livestock across the lake. One of them answered the caller from Claife and returned ashen faced to the small hut where the other ferrymen waited. He died the next day. Whatever he encountered on the High Wray side of the lake must have been horrific – no dog will pass the site of the gibbet and hounds following quarry will stop abruptly and whimper before hurrying away as if from an invisible force.

Along the length of Windermere, it is claimed, travels a ghost ship full of demons, looking for the innocent souls who fall into the lake and drown so they can be taken on board and made members of the crew for eternity.

Wray Castle.

LAKE WINDERMERE, CALGARTH HALL

This beautiful sixteenth-century building was owned by the Cook family until a local magistrate, Myles Philipson, fabricated a lie about the family that led to them being hung for stealing. Philipson had made offers for the property, but the family always refused, so he accused them of stealing his silver cup which he had actually planted in Mr Cook's coat pocket during a meal at the hall. Just before she was led to the gallows, Mrs Cook cursed Philipson and his family, saying that nothing good would come of the lie and that she and her husband would haunt the hall.

On the anniversary of their deaths, two skulls appeared at Calgarth Hall watching the Philipson family. No matter how many times the skulls were buried, burnt, smashed or thrown into Lake Windermere, they always returned to the hall. The Philipson family fell on hard times and the hall, as well as their home and estate, was sold. It was only when the Bishop of Llandaff lived in the hall and performed an exorcism that the hauntings slowed down, appearing now only briefly once every few years. The skulls remain at the hall in a small bricked-up cupboard where they were blessed by the bishop.

On the lake itself is the very strange haunting by a 'Tizzie-Whizzie'. It was during the 1900s that a boatman first saw the creature as he rowed across the lake. He described the creature as having the body of a hedgehog, the tail of a squirrel and the wings of a giant bumblebee. It hovers close to the boat before vanishing in a puff of stinking smoke.

RIVER DARWEN, SAMLESBURY BOTTOM

In the mid-1500s, the daughter of the owner of Samlesbury Hall fell in love with a son of a nearby knight. When the young man approached Sir John, the owner of Samlesbury Hall, he was told angrily that his proposal for marriage would not be accepted because the family had turned their back on the ancestral religion. As the young man left, unhappy and bewildered, the daughter, Lady Dorothy, handed him a note with a map showing where they could continue to meet. With a spring in his step the man walked back to his awaiting carriage.

The couple met clandestinely for many weeks and hatched a plan to elope to one of the young man's father's houses. The day was set. Unfortunately their plans were overheard by Lady Dorothy's brother, who then waited in an ambush as the couple set out to elope. He jumped out of the bushes and shot his sister's suitor and their two companions dead. Their bodies were removed and buried in the nearby chapel, where the ghosts of three people are seen looking down at their graves.

Lady Dorothy was sent abroad to a convent where she went insane, repeating her suitor's name over and over again, eventually dying just one year to the day of their planned elopement, on the anniversary of his murder. For some weeks, the lonely ghost of the young man was seen alone. Upon the death of Lady Dorothy, the figure of a woman dressed in white was said to be seen walking from the hall to the river bank, where she met her lover, dressed in blue armour, and together they strolled hand in hand across the grounds of the estate.

River Douglas, Hesketh Bank

The ghost of Old Man Bailey who died in the mid-1700s is often heard cackling through the area, searching for his son Andrew who, wishing to inherit his father's money sooner rather than later, locked him in the attic of their home and left him to starve to death. Once dead, the body was moved to a bed where the doctor pronounced his death. The son lived on the ill-gained money for a few years, but was haunted by the cackle of his father who would appear to him at all times of the day and night. It was too much for Andrew, who was driven to take his own life in the river.

When clearing out the house for sale, some letters came to light written by Old Man Bailey that confirmed his imprisonment and early death at the hands of Andrew and shed light on the madness that overtook his son.

River Ribble, Peg O'Nell

Be careful when walking by the River Ribble as the ghost of Peg O'Nell may take you to the river bed and add you to the roll-call of his victims.

During the Roman occupation, the river was the site for an annual animal sacrifice, a tradition that carried on until the 1700s. One man who wanted to cross the river before the annual sacrifice had paid the price for his indifference. He walked across the ford, only to be witnessed screaming as two huge arms wrapped around his legs, pulling him deep into the river. He returns to haunt the scene, replaying the ghostly events on the anniversary of his death.

River Ribble, Chingle Hall

This moated manor house, fed by the River Ribble, was originally built in 1260 and later became the birthplace of Father John Wall, a priest who became a Roman Catholic martyr who was executed in 1679 for heresy. His ghost returned after the execution, stomping around the manor, pushing people out of his way and sudden loud noises of cracking timbers could be heard.

Rochdale Canal, Clegg Hall

Clegg Hall was once a magnificent moated hall, home to the Clegg family, and it was from here that Baron de Clegg set off in 1241 to help King Henry fight the French at Poitou. He left his brother, Richard, in charge of his sons whilst he was away, as his wife had died in childbirth. Bertrand and Randulph were like chalk and cheese – Bertrand was the more trusting of the two, whilst Randulph mistrusted his uncle, and with good cause.

As soon as their father had sent word he was on board a ship bound for France, Richard started his campaign to take the family lands for himself, encouraging the boys to go out during the day, where he hoped they would be attacked and killed by one of the marauding gangs in the area. What he had not counted on was the loyalty of the gangs to his brother and his sons. They often returned the boys to the hall at night, having found them wandering in the woods.

One night, Richard waited in the shadows for Bertrand to arrive home after visiting nearby neighbours. Richard had given heavy beer to the guard, who soon went off to sleep, and so the trap was set. As Bertrand sneaked past the sleeping guard he turned to climb the outside steps to his quarters along the wall walk towards the tower, where he stopped to admire the view in the moonlight. As he gazed, his brother, concerned that Bertrand had not returned, went into the courtyard. Looking up he saw his brother and the dark shadow of his uncle with a knife glinting in his hand as he made a strike for Bertrand. Randulph shouted out, 'Brother, beware!' As he ran across the courtyard and up the stairway, he watched his uncle lift the lifeless body of Bertrand into the air before throwing it over the castle wall to fall into the water of the moat.

Randulph fought his uncle, but was no match for the trained soldier who sliced through the boy's body with his sword before throwing him into the moat to join his brother. The next day the guard was paid off and the bodies of the two boys taken from the moat to the chapel, where they rested until burial. Things had not gone well for Baron de Clegg and the King's army, so he returned home heavy hearted and with just one wish, to see his boys.

Awaiting his brother's return, Richard stood at the drawbridge – without the boys – and when he told him they had been slain by a gang of rogues, both the Baron and his horse took on a look of stone. In a fury the Baron banished Richard from the Clegg lands to never set foot on them again lest he be put to death for dishonouring his oath to protect the boys. The Baron then went off to his bed chamber where he stayed, raging against his brother and the world.

Richard, however, had not given up his quest to own the Clegg Estate, and he joined forces with a neighbour, Hubert de Stubbeley, who had been trying to buy the land off the Baron. Richard knew this, so made the offer that if he would help him kill his brother, Richard would give Stubbeley the land he wanted. Stubbeley smiled as he showed Richard a secret door that led to Clegg Castle (Hall). Both families were regularly attacked by gangs until the Baron had made a settlement to them to stop, so in the meantime a tunnel had been dug from Stubbeley Castle to Clegg Castle.

That night, armed with several daggers, Richard went along the tunnel and found the secret door that opened into his brother's chamber. As he lifted a dagger, a voice shouted out, 'Father, Beware!', and as the Baron leapt up from his bed, sword at the ready, he saw a glow in the corner of his room that came closer. It was the dead son, Randulph, who smiled at his father as he pointed to another corner. In the shadows, a tapestry moved back as a figure entered the room, slowly walking towards the bed, knife poised ready to attack. As the figure reached the bed, the moon shone across the bed to show it was empty. As Richard scanned the room, his eyes met those of the ghost, and he screamed in such panic that he did not notice his brother in the room as he ran off down the corridor to the wall walk, from where he plunged into the moat to drown.

Richard's murder of the boys resulted in his body being removed from Clegg land and buried in an unmarked grave. The Baron went on to see the ghosts of both his sons, who would warn him if someone was going to attack him or the castle, and to this day descendants of the Clegg family claim to have heard Randulph's warning.

The hall fell into disrepair over the years, used as an inn between 1818–1896 when it was the Horse and Hounds, haunted by a young girl dressed in a blue dress. She appeared in the older part of the building, and it was only in the late Victorian period that the skeleton of a young girl was found behind a secret door in what must have been the Baron's bedchamber.

LANCASTER CASTLE, LANCASTER CANAL

In 1612 the group of witches later known as the Pendle witches were tried at the Lancaster courts and sentenced to death by hanging – a preferred death sentence to the practice of burning at the stake. The latter method involved the accused being tied up and placed in a large pot of fat which was slowly heated up. As the fire burned, bushels of kindling were thrown on to the screaming victim, igniting the fat, effectively frying the skin and causing almost instant death – if the victim was lucky.

The story of the Pendle witches began when a young member of the coven, Alizon Device, cursed a man who kicked her as she begged for money. She summoned up a demon dog that attacked the man, ripping him limb from limb. A local woman informed the squire about what she

Burning witches.

had witnessed, leading to Device being arrested. Under questioning, she confessed to being a witch and gave the names of twelve other witches in her coven, based at nearby Malkin Tower. The coven were all arrested and charged with the murder of seventeen people in and around the Forest of Pendle. They were also charged with having sold the souls of their victims to familiar spirits or the Devil for earthly gains.

The ghost of Alizon is said to wander Lancaster Castle, holding her head in her hands in realisation of what she had done to her family and friends. If you are on the canal near the castle and see a figure begging, fading in and out of vision, just say hello and pass by, for she has been known to curse people even in death.

STANDEDGE TUNNEL

Standedge Tunnel is Europe's highest and longest tunnel at 3.5 miles, cut through millstone grit that is very resilient. It was completed in 1811. In today's economy, such a feat of engineering would probably cost an estimated £50 million. At the time of its construction, the costs of Standedge Tunnel included the lives of many of the navvies who died during its construction. Passengers often hear their low moans as they sail through the tunnel in convoy, pulled by the British Waterways tug, and see misty figures from the tour boat.

One of the most often reported sightings is that of two human figures struggling with each other towards the middle of the tunnel, silently splashing the water around them. One of the figures is believed to be that of a boat owner who, in 1878, drowned whilst legging his boats through the tunnel with two crew-members. The story the crew-members told when they reached the end of the tunnel – without the owner – was met with suspicion. They claimed they had been legging at the stern of the boat when they were about halfway through Standedge Tunnel. They heard a loud splash, followed by the voice of the boat owner shouting for help. They stopped legging and rushed to the bow of the lead boat, using the light from their oil lamps to illuminate the scene. They heard a few more bangs from under the still moving boats and rushed to the sterns of each boat to see if they could see the owner. They searched for what seemed an age before finally making their way out of the tunnel.

Since each boat was given an allotted time to make their way through the tunnel, the delay was noted and an audience waiting their arrival. Once at the quay they told the tunnel keeper their story. A small boat with the two crew and two others then rowed into the tunnel in search of the owner. They searched for hours, but found nothing. The water is very shallow all the way through Standedge Tunnel and the unlikely story was not believed, but a police constable interviewed the two crewmen and concluded that they were innocent. They apparently had nothing to gain, as the boat was in the owner's name and because he was in debt any assets would go to the money lender.

A few days later, a torrential downpour caused a flash flood through Standedge Tunnel. The boat owner's body was subsequently spotted near the end of the tunnel, with it an unexpected find – the decomposed body of a young woman, around fourteen to fifteen years old, caught up in the clothing of the man. Despite her state of decay it could clearly be seen that her throat had been cut through to the bone. They were both buried in the local church.

It is widely believed that in the tunnel are adits – near horizontal passages through which workmen were lowered from the ground into the tunnel. It was not uncommon for people to meet an untimely end by falling down an adit, and they were commonly used by murderers to hide or dispose of bodies. It is likely that the young girl had been murdered and her body disposed of in this way, only to be released from her watery grave by the sudden rush of water of the flash flood.

The canal steamer *Wasp* was being used to collect workers in the tunnel who were undertaking repairs to its roof in 1871. In the centre was a

Standedge Tunnel.

wooded channel structure, or stank, that only allowed one boat through at a time in order to offer a little safety to the workers. They picked up a carpenter and were making full steam ahead to the other end of the tunnel when they were surprised by a boat being legged towards them; it had sneaked past the tunnel watchman. The crew of the steamer had just stoked up, and the chimney was releasing thick clouds of smoke. In the haze of darkness, they saw the other boat too late and crashed into it with such speed that the boat being legged took on water straight away and the two leggers were killed, crushed between the boats and the stank. The third crew-member was overcome by fumes and died holding the tiller.

The crew of the steamer battled through the wreckage to reach the end of the tunnel. As they made the end they were both overwhelmed by the fumes. One died and fell on to the door of the boiler, resulting in horrific burns. The other was saved when he fell into the canal, the cold water waking him from his stupor. He jumped back on to the steamer and brought her to a stop. The carpenter was also found to have died from fume inhalation.

To this day, many boaters feel they are being watched as they pass through Standedge Tunnel and have heard the harrowing screams of the doomed men, or boggarts as they are popularly known.

LEEDS & LIVERPOOL CANAL – RUFFORD OLD HALL

The Rufford branch of the Leeds & Liverpool Canal has a ghost that walks over a long-since demolished bridge that originally linked Rufford Old Hall to the road into town. Its ghost is seen walking over the phantom bridge in mid-air.

Rufford Old Hall itself has a number of ghosts: there is a man dressed in Elizabethan clothes who paces the garden; Queen Elizabeth I is said to haunt the gallery, and then there is the Grey Lady. It is believed the Grey Lady is the ghost of a young woman in her wedding attire, awaiting the return of her betrothed love who died in battle and never came home. She is seen walking towards the main entrance to the hall.

Rufford Old Hall.

RIVER OUSE, YORK

Along the banks of the River Ouse, near the centre of the city of York, the ghost of a dripping wet woman haunts the area day and night. She looks longingly towards the city centre, as if expecting the arrival of a loved one, before turning and falling into the water.

RIVER URE, SWINTON, YORKSHIRE

The River Ure is haunted by a young lady called Mary at Swinton who died in the 1600s. When Mary's husband began to spend more time with his prize pig than with her, she decided it was about time to get his attention back. Mary stole the pig and drowned it in the river, letting the carcass float off downstream. When her husband came home and found the pig missing he was so outraged he dragged his wife down to the river by her hair. When the pig's carcass was found, he tore Mary's clothes off and drowned her as punishment, letting her body float off down the river. Ever since then, Mary has been seen riding naked on the back of a pig across the river and along the bank near the bridge.

RIVER WHARFE, WHARFEDALE STRIDE

As far back as the spoken word there has been talk of water spirits who will help – or indeed hinder – a traveller wishing to cross the water in which they lived. One such spirit takes the form of a fairy with long green hair who floats gently in the waters of the River Wharfe at Wharfedale Stride. She is seen rising from the dangerous waters on a beautiful white stallion – but beware, if she is seen it is said to be an omen that someone will shortly drown.

HOGGETT'S HOLE, LANGTON, RIVER SWALE

Hoggett's Hole is haunted by Thomas Hoggett, a highwayman who terrorised the Langton area for many years until he met his death in a deep pool in the River Swale. Hoggett was chased by officers of the law across the fields, and when his horse fell from under him he ran towards the river, jumped in and was never seen alive again. His body was recovered a few days later. Ever since, his ghost has haunted the pool and he warns swimmers away from the hidden perils of its waters.

RIVER DOVE, GILLAMOOR

The naked ghost of Kitty Garthwaite is often seen in, or by, the River Dove at Gillamoor, for it was here that she took her own life after a brief affair of the heart with a local squire that resulted in her becoming pregnant. Unmarried mothers were perceived as being almost as bad as the Devil himself, and Kitty Garthwaite was thrown out of her home. Destitute, pregnant and estranged, Kitty walked to Gillamoor where she drowned herself in the river. Beware any young man; Kitty will lure you to join her in her watery grave, turning into a screaming wretch, dragging her victim into the river.

BENINGBOROUGH HALL, RIVER OUSE

In 1670, a local poacher, William Vasey, on the orders of the estate manager Philip Laurie, murdered the beautiful housekeeper of Beningborough Hall. Laurie had, for many years, hoped the housekeeper would become his lover, and was annoyed when he found out that the gamekeeper had called upon her and that they had started to walk out together. The way she met her death was terrible. She was taken from her bed, bound, gagged and thrown into a large sack. After a short trip across the field, the gamekeeper threw the woman into the River Ouse where she was found, still bound in the sack, a little way down the river. Vasey was caught soon after for breaking into a cottage, at which point he confessed to the murder. It was only as he stood on the gallows that he told of the instructions he had received from Laurie. Before he could be captured by an angry mob, Laurie committed suicide with his favourite shotgun.

Both Laurie and the girl are said to haunt the grounds of the now demolished Hall. Laurie's partly decapitated body has been seen on the site of the grounds. The bedraggled figure of a woman pulling at invisible ropes is seen along the river bank.

RIVER SWALE

A black headless dog warns of impending tragedy to families that witness its apparition. The dog haunts the small stone bridge over the River Swale near Muker.

This bridge is part of the Corpse Way, the old route into the village from outlying farms. On the far side of the bridge is a large stone, positioned here to allow coffin bearers to put down their wicker coffins as they took a rest.

RIVER SKELL, FOUNTAINS ABBEY AND STUDLEY ROYAL, YORKSHIRE

This magnificent site, internationally known, boasts a number of ghosts that haunt its buildings and river bank. In the ruins of the abbey, during evening visits, guests and guides have heard the chants of monks at evensong. By the river and around the waterside gardens, a middle-aged couple dressed in late Georgian style stroll as they admire the restored grounds. Watch out for the monk who is seen dashing between the ruins and can appear directly in front of visitors with such abruptness that he has caused some to scream out in panic.

GREAT AYTON, RIVER LEVEN

During the Civil War there were a number of fights in this area, and on one occasion a troop of men were camping near the river for the night when their water was poisoned by a local woman, angry that they had butchered her son and husband the day before. Slipping into the camp, she put the poison into all the water containers she could find, and the rest went into the river. The following day the troop started to wake and the poison soon took hold. The screams of the men and the horses can still be heard in March, and if you dare to look into the river on a moonlit night at this time of year you may see the reflection of the soldiers.

RIVER WHARFE, BOLTON ABBEY

This picturesque twelfth-century ruin is a delight to any artist and the perfect place to see a ghost or two. A monk in a brown cassock walks down the centre of the ruin before turning towards the river, where he vanishes. The rectory is haunted by the same monk, reported by the Revd F.G. Griffiths in 1975, who watched the monk in a hooded brown cassock pass through his dining room before going straight through the wall of that room.

At the river, the ghost of a young woman stands on the stone crossing, beckoning to something unseen.

RIVER WORTH, BLACK BULL, HAWORTH

The Black Bull is over three hundred years old, the inn in which Branwell Brontë, brother of the Brontë sisters, drank away his health after he fell out with his sisters over a manuscript. With the River Worth close by, over the years many a drunk has fallen in the fast-flowing waters and drowned. One of them reportedly stands on the river bank, looking up towards the Black Bull. Inside are said to be a number of ghosts, including a man dressed in beige who sits at a table in the main bar where a girl joins him, offering sweets to someone unseen.

Outside in the car park a young girl sometimes appears, seemingly crying and searching for someone with outstretched arms. An elderly couple walks from the inn out along the road, before disappearing. In room two, a tall dark figure has been seen standing at the bottom of the bed, whilst in room three, the ghost of a maid who took her life after a violent rape still tidies up the room. When the landlady is cleaning, she often hears noises from the empty room and discovers that the hairbrushes inside have been mysteriously placed on the bed.

Glasses drop to the floor yet do not break, the smell of sulpher coal wafts through the inn in the summer when the fires are not lit, and in the bar customers often feel someone brush past them near the painting of the Brontë sisters. Above this picture is a light that is turned sideways overnight, and a bell rings by itself at the bar. Footsteps, muttering and glimpses of a figure walking down a corridor or into the bars have also been described, so next time you visit make sure that you keep your eyes and ears open!

HAVERHOLM PRIORY, LINCOLNSHIRE

A strange little ghost haunts the stone bridge at the end of a long drive at Haverholm Priory. As the unsuspecting target approaches, the ghost whizzes over their head making a strange buzzing noise, likened to that of an angry hornet. Nothing is seen at the bridge, yet at the nearby priory a ghostly monk has been seen and heard walking along a path known locally as 'Ghost Walk'.

BIRKENHEAD, U534

The submarine U534 sits at the Birkenhead ferry terminal, now a multi-million pound tourist attraction. Parts of her hull have been cut away to give visitors a view inside the claustrophobic working environment of a submarine. The story of the U-boat and how she came to be here is a long one that started when her captain refused to surrender on 5 May 1945. She carried on her journey from Denmark to Norway, but later that day was spotted and attacked by the RAF. She received heavy damage and sank by her stern. All but three of the fifty-two crew survived, with five escaping through the torpedo hatch as she lay on the seabed.

The U-boat sat on the bottom of the sea until 1993 when, in August of that year, she was raised with much speculation that she held Nazi treasure. No treasures were found as such, but a fully functioning Enigma machine was discovered. She was put on show at the Birkenhead Submarine Museum before being moved to her new site. Even before she was moved, staff and visitors had seen two figures inside the submarine – one near the periscope, a man gesturing to his crew, the other in the torpedo room, where three of the most advanced torpedoes were discovered, with wiring to suggest someone was trying to blow it up.

ASTLEY, MANCHESTER

Along the towpath of the canal wanders the figure of a lone woman, Ann Mort, searching for her murdered lover. Ann Mort had fallen deeply in love with a Catholic man, which did not find favour with her proudly Protestant family who were very keen for the union to end. Ann and her lover planned to elope, but unbeknown to them they had been overheard by a servant, who immediately reported back to her family. Ann's father and brother caught the couple and murdered the young Catholic man before burying his body on what would later become the line of the canal. Ann was confined to a garret room, where she died of a broken heart. The house was later demolished to make way for the canal, and it is in this area that Ann walks the towpath in search of her lost love.

SALTERSFORD TUNNEL, TRENT & MERSEY CANAL

Saltersford Tunnel, which began construction in 1775 and saw its first death that same year, is claimed to be the most haunted tunnel of all the waterways in Britain. It has built up such a reputation that no boater would dare travel through it alone. There are tales of sudden deafening screams, banging on the roof and sides of the boats, boats pulled and pushed by invisible hands and lights in the tunnel appearing through the walls and ceiling.

Are they the ghosts of the many men who perished in this and other tunnels throughout the waterways system?

BUTTERMILK BRIDGE, SANKEY CANAL

When the canal was being built, an old crone would visit the navvies daily to make her living by selling them her buttermilk. Her ghost is seen on the Buttermilk Bridge, dressed in a long black cloak with a frightening pointed face and a cackle that echoes along the canal banks. She died on the newly built bridge as she sold her buttermilk, and returns there to collect her pales.

MACCLESFIELD CANAL, LYME PARK, CHESHIRE

From 1346 the hall within Lyme Park was the home of the Legh family, bestowed upon Sir Piers Legh for rescuing the standard of the Black Prince, and it remained in the family until 1946, when it was given to the National Trust in lieu of death duties. The ghost of a woman walks the route of the funeral cortège of the younger Sir Piers Legh, son of the first Sir Piers Legh, who died of his wounds at the Battle of Meux in 1422 where he fought alongside King Henry V. The ghost proceeds along the river bank and across the canal built many years later, continuing towards Stockport. She is believed to be Sir Piers's mistress, who was banned from attending the funeral by the family who told her never to enter the estate again. She died of a broken heart, her body found lying next to her lover's tomb on the estate.

CHESTER, SHROPSHIRE UNION CANAL (THE SHROPPIE)

At the northern end of the Shropshire Union Canal sits Chester, where the ghost of a Roman centurion is seen. He first appeared when the canal was being dug in the late eighteenth century. The navvies had cut through a wall extending across the path of the canal from the town wall. The centurion appears to stand guard alongside the canal, near Water Tower Street, and he has occasionally been seen to walk across the canal along an invisible wall.

RIVER NOE, EDALE

In the 1700s, a young boy was murdered in dreadful circumstances; like Oliver Twist in Dickens's novel, he had asked for more food from his cruel guardian. He was dragged to the river's edge, thrashed over the head with a blunt instrument and thrown into the cold waters below. Every year, in March, the sound of a boy screaming is followed by dull thuds, dragging and then the noise of something being thrown into the river.

MOIRA, DERBYSHIRE

At the restored Napoleonic blast furnace on the edge of Moira is a section of the Ashby-de-la-Zouch Canal, built in 1804 and reopened so that pleasure trips could continue to the nearby National Forest Centre in 2001. In the building of the Moira Furnace a number of ghosts were described, including that of a small boy crouching in a corner of the upper floor that leads to the mouth of the furnace. During the short life of the production of iron there, there were a number of accidents involving women and young children who had the dangerous job of feeding the furnace. It was not uncommon for them to be pulled to their deaths by the weight of the wheelbarrow and its contents of iron ore, coke or limestone as they tipped it into the open mouth of the furnace. One

Moira Furnace.

Moira furnace and canal.

slip and they tumbled to what would be a certain death from asphyxiation, before becoming part of the next batch of cast iron. Moira Furnace has become a popular site for paranormal investigations and often holds ghost hunts.

RIVER TRENT, SWARKESTONE BRIDGE

The first crossing of this area of marshland either side of the River Trent was built in the thirteenth century to prevent the river spirit taking more souls. Two beautiful sisters of the Bellmont family had been throwing a party to celebrate their joint engagement to two brothers when the men were summoned to the other side of the valley for a meeting of the barons. While the two sisters waited for their men to return, a storm blew up and the river flooded. The brothers made their way to the ford and gallantly tried to cross the swollen river on horseback. As they reached the centre of the river, a huge monster rose up from the waters and carried the men away to their deaths. When the sisters heard the news they commissioned the building of a bridge in memory of their lost loves. They never married and spent their fortune on the upkeep of the bridge, eventually dying so poor that they were buried in the same grave. Whenever there is a storm and the river is swollen, the two sisters are said to stand on the bridge looking out across the marsh as if searching for their fiancés.

Swarkerstone Bridge.

SADDINGTON TUNNEL

Saddington Tunnel, built in 1797, has a ghost that is heard crying out for help, yet there are no records to show whom it could be. As with the construction of any tunnel, there were many accidents in which a great number of men and boys died.

NEWARK CASTLE

From the River Trent, the majesty of Newark Castle towers above the landscape and, despite its ruinous condition, still commands the river and surrounding area.

The ghost of King John is believed to haunt the castle ruins for it was here, at midnight one night in 1216, that he died in agony during a violent storm. In recent years, various paranormal hunters have tried to capture King John's ghost. They have been met with other-worldly hostility; bright lights blind their vision and stones have been thrown at them. It would seem the castle and her ghosts do not want to give up their secrets just yet.

As you travel along the river, look up at the castle and you may catch a glimpse of the ghost of a child who looks longingly out of a top floor window.

THE EMBANKMENT CLUB

The former Boots Social Club, now known as the Embankment Club, claims the ghost of Jessie Boot, the local philanthropist who paid for the building and helped many people in the poorest areas of Nottingham. It is said that during any building work that is undertaken, and for some time after, Jessie Boot paces the corridors to check the building is safe.

Newark Castle.

A short distance from the canal, the spectre of a drowned child clings to the bridge arch before vanishing.

RIVER ISE, BARTON SEAGRAVE

The story of Lady Isobel, who died of a broken neck when her horse threw her into the river bank near her home at Barton Seagrave, dates back to the fourteenth century. Her ghost walks from the village towards the river and then appears to float above the flowing water in a manner that suggests she does not want her shoes to get wet. The best time to see her is on a fine winter evening as the sun is setting and the low mists are rising.

CHRISTINA COLLINS, TRENT & MERSEY CANAL

On 17 June 1839 a young woman, Christina Collins, was murdered by three boatmen after they had been drinking in a local pub. Christina had the misfortune to be walking across a field at Brindely Bank, where she was spotted by boatmen who had stopped on their way back to their boats on the Trent & Mersey Canal. After they had repeatedly raped the young woman, her throat was cut and her body thrown into the canal. Her screams were heard in the village, but a rescue party arrived too late to save her. As her sodden body was pulled from the canal, a flow of blood oozed from her wound and trickled down the sandstone steps to the canal. The three men were caught trying to escape on their boats and were sent to trial. Emotion was running high in the village and a mob surrounded the prison, wanting revenge for the killing of Christina. Two of the men received death sentences whilst the third, found to be a bystander, was transported to Australia.

To this day, a pitiful image of a young woman has been seen on balmy summer evenings looking across the canal to the field in which she was attacked. A bloodstain appears on the stone steps and lingers for a few days before disappearing.

The lady in the canal.

CHAPTER FOUR

MIDDLE ENGLAND

LITTLE ONN, SHROPSHIRE UNION CANAL

At Little Onn, near Church Eaton in Staffordshire on the Shropshire Union Canal (or the Shroppie, as it is affectionately known), the ghost of an American pilot can sometimes be seen. He crashed his plane beside the canal and was thrown to a watery death. He is seen rising from the centre of the canal or falling head first into the flames of his burning aircraft.

SHROPSHIRE UNION CANAL

At the top of Adderley Locks, past Bridge 66, is the haunted Brownhills Wood, where a man is seen walking along the towpath apparently talking to himself – yet he is never heard. He is dressed in the style of a parson from the seventeenth century, perhaps on his way to give a sermon that was never to be?

BADGER DINGLE, SHROPSHIRE

This well-known beauty spot once formed part of the gardens of the larger Badger Estate, designed to make use of the steep-sided valley with the

High Bridge, Grub Street cutting, the Shroppie.

Snowdon Brook running through it. The hall is long since gone, but the dingle remains as a reminder of the grand designs on the estate. There is even a restored folly temple available to rent. At the bottom of the dingle is a series of pools that appear romantic in the daylight, but at night they take on a more sinister appearance.

Grub Street cutting.

Several people have met a man walking through the dingle late at night. He chats about the local inn and the girl there he loves, before vanishing into the dark. Shortly down the way, on approaching the bottom pool, a glowing shape rises up out of it and passers by have felt as if they were being pulled towards the pool's edge. Many believe this to be the ghost of Dick Dulson, a man who committed suicide in the pool one Christmas Eve after he failed to win the hand of his beloved, the girl from the nearby inn.

BOMERE POOL

Take a walk along the edge of Bomere Pool on the eve of Easter Sunday, and you may see a Roman soldier rowing a coracle across the pool, which was once connected to a river. He is rowing in search of his love, who drowned alongside him as they tried to escape from an angry local mob who were against the marriage of a Roman soldier to one of their women.

The area is also known for having a wicked community which once corrupted the minister who was sent to bring them closer to God. On Christmas Eve, one minute before midnight, when the minister was drinking and enjoying the pleasures of a local woman instead of reading his sermon from the pulpit, there was a mighty crashing noise and the whole village was engulfed by a flash flood that took them 'to the bottom of the world'. If you are brave enough to visit at midnight on this day, you can hear the minister preaching to the wicked people of his parish from deep below the surface of the pool.

CRICK

The area of Crick has a number of ghostly goings-on. The tunnel is home to the ghost of a woman who is sometimes confused with Kit Crewbucket of Harecastle Tunnel fame, and with the female ghost who haunts the Saltersford Tunnel. This ghostly woman is sometimes seen in the water for a brief second. People mooring between the tunnel mouth and the first bridge towards Crick have described seeing the bedraggled figure of a young woman who has no face, just a pale glow where her features should be. A local man walking his dog on the towpath suddenly became aware that the dog had frozen to the spot and was growling at something ahead. The man could not see anything himself but did notice that the air had become very cool. His dog refused to move past the spot, and despite the man's attempts to pull him along, he slipped his collar and ran back towards the road.

In the tunnel, some boaters have seen what appears to look like a boat approaching them from the opposite direction. Slowing down in order to pass, they have watched, astonished, as the boat and light slowly disappear into the gloom of the tunnel.

Edwards, an award-winning restaurant, was once the warehouse and stable for the canal, and it is in the restaurant that staff have heard footsteps, seen shadowy figures moving about the room and even cutlery move across tables, as if pushed by an invisible hand.

The canal circles around Cracks Hill, and from the summit the line of the canal is visible as well as fine views to Crick and beyond. On the summit are the remains of a Roman fort, from where a number of Roman centurions leave to patrol the land around and have been reported to walk straight across the canal on a route they used long before canal or road was built.

CRICK TUNNEL AND HARECASTLE TUNNEL, KIDSGROVE, GRAND UNION CANAL

In 1839 a woman who worked the boats as companion and cook was murdered and her decapitated body thrown into the waters of the tunnel, where it was found days later. Since then a boggart (a household, or in this case tunnel, fairy) appears. She is Kit Crewbucket, the dead woman who was found in the water. Her party trick is that, should she like you, she will cook you a hearty breakfast, the smell of frying bacon filling the tunnel.

Be warned, though, if she takes a dislike to you she will scream, so they say, until you go mad. For some unknown reason, the ghostly cook also appears in the Harecastle Tunnel with her breakfast menu on offer.

HARECASTLE TUNNEL

Harecastle Tunnel is the site of a true, but misty, tale. During the research undertaken for this book, the author received many stories about ghostly encounters, this one from Richard Smith:

Ursula.

In September 1994 I was making my way, single-handedly, northwards on the Trent & Mersey Canal on my narrow-boat, *Ursula,* en route from base at Sawley to Ellesmere Port. I had stopped overnight at Hem Heath, despite the usual attempts at intimidation by the local youths, and so Tuesday 27 September saw me setting off about 08.00, on a fine mild morning.

Anyone who has boated single-handedly will know that there are two snags which are rarely mentioned in literature on the matter, one being the obvious need to plan ahead to put the kettle on, and the other, the less obvious need to plan ahead to deal with the consequences of previous cuppas. It seemed to me that the inevitable wait at the south end of Harecastle Tunnel would enable me to deal with both matters easily, and in comfort, but it was not to be.

As I came round the last gentle bend at the south end (the log book shows at 11.29), there were no boats waiting; after a moment's hesitation the tunnel keeper appeared and waved me briskly forward into the tunnel, I presumed – correctly – more or less on the tail end of the convoy that had just entered. So, no cuppa, no personal-needs break, and no idea what sort of boat was next in line in front of me. So, straight into the tunnel, and as usual the doors closed behind me and the fan came on.

An immediate result was a mist in the tunnel, as the warm moist air from the north end was sucked into the cold, and reduced visibility as a consequence. I was hurrying a bit to tag on to the convoy, and so was catching up with the boat in front and of course eased down. It became clear that I was still catching up, so I slowed even more, so that I hardly had steerage, until eventually I realised that the other boat had stopped in front of me.

I could see through the mist that the boat was a working motor, beautifully painted and with a full set of whitened rope work – but there was no one at the tiller. The boat was as askew across the tunnel as a full-length boat could be – in other words some, but not much, stern to the right and bow to the left. The very flat angle meant that I could not see any name or ownership on the cabin sides.

I decided that I couldn't wait any longer, so having come to a stop I decided to pop to the loo on the way through the boat, then go to the front and give a shout to see what the problem was, and how I might help. I put this plan into action, but when I reached the front of my boat there was no mist and no stationary boat – the tunnel being perfectly clear, and the only other boat a long way away towards the Kidsgrove end. I wasn't scared, and there was no sensation of anything strange, but I decided I'd better get a good move on, otherwise a search party would be triggered on the assumption that I had broken down.

The log shows that I cleared the north end at 12.30, so the passage had taken me an hour rather than the usual forty-five minutes, and this despite the fact that I had put in some fast boating after the mist cleared to catch up.

I can see that boat as clearly now in my mind's eye as I saw it in 1994. I had long-since read about Kit Crewbucket, but was then, and am still now, entirely open-minded about ghosts. I am reporting honestly exactly what I saw – this isn't fiction! Retirement has given me time I did not have before to put the story on paper. I did not report it at the time, in case someone thought I was making it up.

SHROPSHIRE UNION CANAL

On the Shropshire Union Canal, in the short tunnel at Ellesmere that leads into the town close to a former lengthman's cottage, is another tunnel ghost. This ghost belongs to a woman whose body was found in the tunnel as a boat was being legged through, her body having become jammed between the boat and the tunnel wall. Partly naked, the woman's body was pulled up on deck and taken back towards Ellesmere. As no one knew who she was, she was buried by the parish in an unmarked grave. To this day, on crisp winter evenings, people travelling through the canal have seen someone jump onto the boat before any stoppages, yet the figure falls straight through into the water. Did she commit suicide, or was she murdered?

Further along the canal – reputed to be the most haunted in the country – is Bridge 39, haunted by a black shadowy figure that looks like a big monkey with large eyes. One sighting was reported by a labourer hired to take luggage from Ranton to Newport in January 1879. He was carrying out his task when, at Bridge 39, he claimed to see a big, black, shaggy-haired monkey with enormous eyes jump on to the back of his horse in an attempt to steal it. The man struck out at the shape but was so frightened when he saw his whip cut right through it that he fell to the floor, the horse bolting with the figure clinging to it. The labourer took to his bed for several days, and when he did return to Bridge 39 he found his whip still lay where he had dropped it. What he had seen was known locally as the monkey man, who was said to be the spirit of a boatman drowned under Bridge 39.

A more recent sighting led to much amusement when a father at the helm of a boat saw the 'monkey man' and shouted to his family, who were in the galley, to come and look at the beast. He was the only one to see the ghost, and he became the laughing stock of his family. The father appealed to the Waterways Trust for information, who confirmed there had been similar sightings at Bridge 39.

BETTON CUTTING, MARKET DRAYTON, SHROPSHIRE UNION CANAL

During the building of the canals at Betton Cutting there were many accidents, often resulting in death. An unfortunate navvy was crushed under a truck full of stones that fell on him as he dug away at the bottom of the cutting at Betton, near Market Drayton. His screams can still be heard at night, fading away as a figure is seen walking along the towpath.

TYRLEY LOCKS, SHROPSHIRE UNION CANAL

Passing Market Drayton at night and entering the Tyrley Locks, you may be helped along at the middle lock by a friendly ghost who will happily close the gates behind you!

Tyrley Locks.

WILLEYMOOR, SHROPSHIRE UNION CANAL

A first-hand account from Jean Cross:

I read with interest your article in the *Towpath Telegraph* and it took me back to an incident I had experienced in the early 1990s on the Shropshire Union Canal.

We had just come through the lock at Willeymoor and moored up on the Grindley side as we had decided to eat out that night. At three o'clock in the morning, I was woken up by the sound of an approaching animal galloping rather fast. As the noise grew louder and louder, I opened the curtains to get a look at the idiot who was galloping at that late hour along the towpath. I should have seen the rider pass the boat as the noise grew really loud, but there was absolutely nothing and the noise stopped instantaneously. I was rather bemused by this and grabbed the torch and went out into the cratch area. There was still nothing to be seen. There was nothing in the field behind and the night was calm and still. Neither my husband or children had heard anything and slept through it all.

My family thought I was mad when I recalled my moonlit experience of the night, and even joked and accused me of having drunk one too many at the pub. As I only ever drink a half of lager and lime, this was not the case. So it remains a mystery to this day. Had I heard an escaped horse out for a run? Hardly, as I would have seen it. Was it a deer? Unlikely, as the animal sounded as if it was shod and again I didn't see it. Or could it have been some phantom rider, desperate to get to somewhere? I will never know. But to be on the safe side, we have never moored overnight there since.

CHILDS ERCALL POOL

Legend goes that a mermaid was captured at sea and brought to live in the pool at Childs Ercall by her captor, an old sea captain. He treated her well, but when he died she was so upset at the way she was treated by his relations that she swam to the bottom of the pool and never returned. It was thought that she guarded the old captain's treasure that had never been found after his death. She is often heard singing at the bottom of Childs Ercall pool on balmy summer evenings.

ELLESMERE

The mere itself is home to the ghost of an old woman, Mrs Ellis, who inherited the meadow in which stood a well, the only source of water for the town and where people would fill up their buckets free of charge. However,

Ellesemere Basin.

Mrs Ellis was a greedy woman, and she decided to charge the townsfolk a farthing for filling the buckets with water, resulting in the poor of the parish suffering needlessly. They went to the vicar, who prayed for fresh water to be free for the poor, and in answer, during the second night of the ban, the water rose up, flooding the meadow and drowing the wicked Mrs Ellis. The whole of her house, meadow and valley was under water and lost to the mere for all time. If you stand at the edge of the mere at night you may hear the screams of Mrs Ellis as she frantically tries to bail the water out of her home.

At the shore of the mere, from Oteley Park, a woman in white walks with her head covered. Be careful – should she look up at you then you are said to go mad and throw yourself into the dark waters of Ellesmere.

Ellesmere Tunnel.

Haunted Ellesmere Tunnel.

BERWICK WHARF, ATCHAM

During the 1950s a small camp had been established on the disused Second World War airfield. Most people living there were hard working and willing to turn their hand to anything to make a living and keep the peace with the local communities. They were quickly accepted, and some of the local youngsters would babysit for their new neighbours. On one such occasion, a young girl was babysitting for a man with three children. He had gone to the pub with a group from the camp, later saying that he felt unwell and returning home. He was sweet on the young girl babysitting for him, and thought she felt the same way about him. He had been drinking and did not take kindly to her somewhat disdainful dismissals of his advances.

In a rage he raped her before strangling her. Realising what he had done, he gathered up his victim, her clothes, shoes and handbag and disposed of them all in a nearby air shaft of the old Shropshire Canal. He continued on to the pub where, in an attempt to provide an alibi, he said he had seen some men walking toward the commune with sticks. When the group arrived home, two of them offered to take the babysitter home across the fields. When she could not be found they thought that she must have gone home early, leaving the children unattended. It was not until her parents and the local police visited that the community knew something was wrong.

The police searched the area, but missed the air shaft, and interviewed everyone at the camp. The killer managed to convince the police that he had had too much to drink. He claimed to have been violently sick outside the pub, in the fields looking across to the camp, when he had seen the men and then gone back in to tell the others. He must have thought he had got away with it, as the days and weeks passed without her body being found.

A local man was out walking his dog one day when he noticed a young woman sitting on the old brick canal air shaft, brushing her long hair. Being somewhat tipsy he thought nothing of it and went home to bed. The next morning he told his wife what he had seen, but she dismissed his story by making the hand gesture of holding a drink. That night, the *Shropshire Star* published a photograph of the girl, but in the picture she had shorter hair than the vision the man had seen by the air shaft. He contacted the police, a little concerned that he might be wasting their time. They sent a policeman around to take down some more details, and it was the fact that he had seen her with longer hair that proved to be a vital clue. The photograph in the paper was a few years old, and the girl had since let her hair grow long in the style of the day. He took the search party to the air shaft and a policeman was lowered down on a rope. Just a few yards inside the canal tunnel were what looked like a pile of old clothes. It was not until the policeman got to a boat that he realised the bundle was actually the body of the murder victim. However, there were no DNA testing techniques at the time, and all evidence of the murderer had been washed away in the canal water.

A few weeks later, however, the murderer gave himself up, apparently driven to admitting his guilt by the sight of the girl standing at the end of his bed, dripping wet and beckoning him to follow her.

THE OLD WAREHOUSE, RIVER SEVERN

The old warehouse, built in 1838, is a fine example of Gothic revival architecture, with its imposing turrets and battlements. The main purpose of the building was as a loading and unloading base for the Severn trows travelling up and down the river from Bristol. It is now the museum of the river for the Ironbridge Gorge Museum Trust. In front of the building is a slipway, with tracks that were used to guide the wagons that travelled between the trows and the warehouse. During the early morning rush, when safety was a secondary consideration, children were used as brakemen, putting blocks under the wagon to stop them rolling too fast down the incline to the waiting trows. A young lad who had been working through the night to unload a number of trows was sleepy, and he did not hear the warning cry from his gang master. He struggled to pull his block from under the wagon he was attempting to stop. A runaway wagon, full of off-loaded goods, hit the boy and swept him to his death, crushing him between the wagon and the sailing barge. His tragic little figure is sometimes seen pulling at his invisible block before vanishing.

THE IRONBRIDGE, RIVER SEVERN

The Ironbridge was the first bridge in the world to be constructed of iron, and is now the central feature in the world heritage site. The bridge is made using the same design techniques as a wooden bridge, but using iron 'pegs' to hold the iron structure together. Below the bridge flows the River Severn, out towards Bristol and the sea.

The Ironbridge phantom.

In the dead of night, silently shrouded in a mist, a boat similar in shape and size to a Severn trow glides slowly down the river towards Jackfield, where it is seen tied up and unloading its secret cargo. At the helm stands a tall figure with a hood covering his features. Upon the deck and in the hold is a gruesome cargo of bodies. During the fifteenth and sixteenth centuries, plague-ridden bodies were collected and buried in lime-lined pits to contain the disease. People who had developed immunity to the plague were employed to help move the bodies either to a pyre, or to transport them for removal to a burial pit.

FERRY ROAD, JACKFIELD, RIVER SEVERN

During the winter months the River Severn rises and becomes a treacherous body of water. It was at such a time that young twins were playing on the spoil heaps from the Craven–Dunhill Tile Works. The recent heavy rain had made the spoil heap unstable and it collapsed as the twins played on it, plunging them into the river. They drowned as they were swept away, their bodies snared in a tree that had been washed downriver and caught under the footbridge a few yards further on. Following an exhaustive search they were spotted, and their tiny bodies recovered from the river still holding hands. They were taken to the first cottage in Ferry Road. To this day the children have been seen splashing in the river in front of the bridge and heard crying for their mother along the small road and in the garden of the first house in the stretch of terraces.

APLEY POOL, WELLINGTON

On 9 February 1883, the head of a young girl was found on the shore of Apley Pool stuffed into a sack, a discovery that bought to light one of the most horrific murders of the nineteenth century.

In the small village of Kynnersley lived Polly Mayas, along with her father Richard, her stepmother Elizabeth and three of Elizabeth's children. Polly was not wanted by Elizabeth, and was often seen by her neighbours neglected and starving for both food and affection. Her father worked long hard hours to keep the family fed, and often Polly was already in bed when he came in from work, so he did not notice his daughter's decline at the hands of his new wife. Elizabeth often beat Polly, the neighbours frequently stepping in to stop the attacks.

During one particularly harsh beating Polly was knocked out cold, and later died from a fractured skull. In panic, Elizabeth cut up her body and tried to burn it. When that did not work she put the body parts into sacks and gave them to her husband to dump under the pretence that they were kitchen waste. The neighbours feared the worst when Polly vanished and were told by Elizabeth that she had gone to an institution in Shrewsbury where she would be taught a trade. They all believed her, even Polly's father who had unknowingly taken her broken body and thrown it into Apley Pool on his way to work, believing the contents of the sacks to be just rubbish.

Elizabeth had told her husband that Polly would be released from the institution when she was sixteen, having learned to be a seamstress, and that no contact with her was allowed. Polly's father believed his new wife and was completely crushed when he found out the truth, and the added horror that he had thrown his daughter's body into the pool.

Once the facts about Polly's murder came to light the cottage was ransacked by an angry mob and all of Elizabeth's clothes burnt in the street. Extra police officers were drafted in to stop Wellington Police Station from being over-run, such was the outrage of the local people. When the police tried to drive a horse-drawn carriage through the crowds with the couple inside, the mob nearly turned the carriage over and mounted police had to clear the way.

Due to the high level of outrage, the two were committed for trial at Stafford where Mr Justice Stephens heard the case on 26 April 1883. Polly's father was acquitted of murder, but given eighteen months' hard labour for being an accessory after the fact. Elizabeth was said to have mental problems and so was given twenty years for manslaughter, but died within six years of her imprisonment.

What is most strange are the circumstances in which the head was first found. Two poachers out along the banks of Apley Pool saw a young girl paddling in the shallows of the pool. As they approached her their dogs began to bark at a sack floating in some reeds nearby. Distracted, they took their eyes off the girl for a second to see what was exciting the dogs. Imagine the shock of opening the soaking wet sack to see the partially burnt head of the girl looking up at them!

BIRMINGHAM CANAL NAVIGATION

At Black Path Park, Smethwick, the ghost of an old woman is seen walking along the towpath dressed in a bonnet and red cape before vanishing in front of nearby walkers' eyes. She is believed to be the ghost of a nurse who would tend the boat families on the canal. Her kindness was repaid when she passed away, as at the time of her funeral all the horns on the boats in the area tooted as a mark of respect.

WAST HILLS TUNNEL, WORCESTER & BIRMINGHAM CANAL

Wast Hills Tunnel is one of the longest tunnels in the country and boasts the spectre of a ghostly working boat that appears out of nowhere before disappearing into the mists of the passageway. The tunnel is interesting in that it has a slight bend in it, and at mid-point neither entrance nor exit can be seen – just blackness.

Several people have reported seeing a figure of a woman standing on the bow of their boat, pointing to the end of the tunnel as if warning of something approaching. She turns with a look of terror before melting into the gloom of the tunnel.

Before steam tugs these tunnels were very dangerous places for the leggers who would walk the boats through the tunnels. As conditions were so poor and the pain caused by everyday legging was so intense the men would drink between jobs, often resulting in their falling into the canal. If they could swim, or at least hang on to the boat, they would be fine. Others, however, were not so lucky and drowned, their wavering cries for help going unheeded by the generations of canal users.

NETHERTON TUNNEL, BIRMINGHAM CANAL NAVIGATIONS

The Netherton Tunnel was built between 1855 and 1858. Nine men perished during a roof fall and it took days to recover their bodies. The

The author at the helm of narrow-boat *Great Western*.

remains of at least three were left where they had been buried by the fall. Boaters hear cries of pain and anguish that fill the tunnel without warning, the air goes cold and then an eerie silence falls, when only the noise of the engine from the moving boat can be heard. There have also been sightings of figures milling around the entrance of the tunnel, before melting into its structure.

TARDIBIGGE, WORCESTER & BIRMINGHAM CANAL

The tunnel at Tardibigge, opened on 30 March 1807, is reputedly haunted by two leggers who drowned there after falling off the boat they were taking through it. The men would spend their waiting time drinking in the public house that stood above the mouth of the Tardibigge Tunnel, buying pints with the money they had earned from previous jobs. Many of the men lived in a shanty-style village that had sprung up in fields nearby, and their wives had to be quick to grab the money for food before the men went to the inn to refresh themselves with a beer – or three – before their next trip.

After three men drowned in the same week, the Earl of Plymouth, who owned much of the land in the area, closed down the inn and championed the use of steam tugs to pull boats through the tunnel. A footpath links both sides of the canal and it is said that one of the unfortunate men can be seen running from the mouth of the canal and up over the hill towards the encampment at Tardibigge. In the tunnel itself, as well as the occasional splash made by the stone of the tunnel breaking away, there can be heard a low sob of someone crying and there have been sightings of a ghostly working boat.

A funny incident took place one Halloweeen when a boatman from the Alvechurch end of the tunnel decided to top up his water tank at Tardibigge. Halfway through the tunnel he saw a floating castle and, knowing of the story of the ghost boat and its men, closed his eyes and steered ahead – only to hit a butty that had been dressed as a haunted castle for an event at Tardibigge. Fortunately no damage was done, except to some paintwork and possibly his pride!

In the old post office, a woman has been seen at the back of the building counting money and stamping an invisible letter or similar piece of paperwork. The top lock, which is claimed to be the deepest lock in the country, is haunted by a lock keeper who tends the garden of the nearby cottage and is sometimes seen by the lock gates. Further down the canal are the remains of three butties left to rot after the collapse of the canal trade. Sat on the stern of the middle butty is the ghost of a boatman, checking the way forward and waving to someone ahead of him.

DUDLEY TUNNEL

Dudley Tunnel lies next to the award-winning Black Country Living Museum and is reputedly haunted by many ghosts of times past. Despite this it has a happy atmosphere. Many people who steer the pleasure boats in and out of Dudley Tunnel tell of hearing a soft voice which says things like, 'nicely done' and 'that was easy.' In the huge caverns that link to the canal, shadows flit from place to place and unexpected laughter rings out. The museum itself claims a number of ghosts who haunt the reconstructed building.

In the toll keeper's cottage, a woman is often seen sitting in the chair near the fire as visitors wander around the museum. In the foundry, a man walks around inspecting the machines, while another wanders around the lime kilns, and in the bakery a woman is often seen out in the back rooms. On the canal bank is the butty, *Diamond*, who sits partly covered by a shed awaiting restoration. Sitting on its stern is the ghost of an old boatman who visits her on a regular basis. Perhaps he is a past owner checking on her condition and keeping her company, as it is widely believed that every boat – especially wooden ones – have souls that need to be cherished.

RYTON BRIDGE, RIVER AVON

A local highwayman, Thomas Wildey, was hung for the murder of a mother and daughter on 2 May 1734. Thomas Wildey was a woolcomber who carried out a savage attack on the women. The murders had taken place on Ryton Bridge on the River Avon and the bodies were so badly dismembered that it took some hours to work out who they were. Wildey was left hanging in an iron gibbet cage at nearby Whitley Common, a grisly warning to all who passed.

People passing over the bridge have often reported seeing the figure of a man surrounded in mist accompanied by the smell of rotting flesh. Down by the river the pitiful ghostly figure of a mother has been seen defending her daughter against an unseen assassin before fading away, whilst under the arch of the bridge lights have been reported flitting on the underside surface.

TAMWORTH, RIVER TRENT

Two ghosts haunt Tamworth Castle, on the banks of the River Trent. The first is that of the Lady in Black, who is apparently Editha, sister of King Athelstan, who gave her away to Sihtric, the Danish King of Northumbria, in the early tenth century. Although he had promised to become a Christian, he reverted to his pagan ways and left Editha for another woman. Editha was broken-hearted and spent the rest of her life in the convent she founded to do good for the people of the area. After her death the convent thrived, along with the nearby Polesworth, until William the Conqueror gave the convents to Robert de Marmion, who immediately threw the nuns out.

One night soon afterwards, as Marmion tried to get to sleep, he became aware that someone was in his room. It was the ghost of Editha, who struck him with her crozier as she told him that if he did not repent and allow the nuns back to Polesworth he would pay a high price, with his soul being damned to hell upon his tortured death. The cut was deep to his head, and as he staggered down the stairs blood gushed from the wound onto the stone steps. He repented, but the Lady in Black frequently returns to keep an eye on her property.

The second ghost is a Lady in White, the lover of Sir Tarquin who had a reputation for being a cruel punisher of servants and fellow knights alike. One day, she looked on as Sir Lancelot killed her lover on Lady Meadow, below the castle, before freeing some forty captured knights in various states of torture. Such was the distress she felt when she saw the cruelties her lover had heaped on the knights that she threw herself from the curtained wall where she had been watching events below. Many strange noises have been heard within the castle, both by day and night.

ODDINGLEY, THE WORCESTER & BIRMINGHAM CANAL

The small village of Oddingley lies between Worcester and Droitwich, through which the Worcester & Birmingham Canal runs. Oddingley was the scene of two murders in June 1806. A local carpenter, Richard Hemming, shot the Revd G. Parker, the rector of the parish of St James, at point-blank range. Following the murder, Hemming was never seen again. He was known to be a violent man and to have fallen into debt after gambling with a group of four local men; a debt that he was unable to pay. But why had he brutally murdered the rector?

Revd G. Parker was an unpopular man. He was disliked for extracting every penny of tithe tax from his parishioners, and was even known to take livestock without consent to sell at market if he felt a full tithe had not been paid. He was hated across the parish. Four local men – Clewes, Banks, Bennett and Taylor – hatched a plan to get rid of the reverend once and for all, and hired Hemming to commit the murder as a way of paying off his debt. The scheme was set: as Parker drove a heard of cows down a narrow lane for milking, Hemming would shoot him.

All went to plan and the reverend was fatally shot by Hemming, who had hidden in nearby bushes to wait for his quarry. Leaving his gun behind, Hemming doubled back to the village where Clewes persuaded him to hide in the hayloft of his barn at Netherwood Farm. The conspirators, afraid that Hemming would reveal their involvement, agreed that he would have to die. Clewes, Banks, Bennett and Taylor lured Hemming out of his hiding place with the offer of food and beer. As soon as he was in sight they set about him, beating him to death before burying him under the floor of the old barn.

Once the reverend's body was discovered the musket found nearby was recognised as belonging to Hemming and a wide search was ordered. After a few days the search was halted, and it was assumed that he had fled the country. An inquest was held at Talbot Inn in nearby Barnbourne, where the conspirators were charged with murder. Clewes confessed, but the verdict was found not guilty due to lack of evidence. On a cold winter's day, some twenty-four years later, Hemming's body was located buried under the floor of the barn at Netherwood Farm.

As both Hemming and Revd Parker met a sudden end, it is no surprise that their ghosts have appeared close to their places of death. The rector has been seen getting up from the road and walking down towards the canal bridge that carries Netherwood Lane. Hemming stands around the buildings of the farm, raising his arms as if to defend himself from invisible blows, before fading away.

In the neighboring hamlet of Dunhamstead, the Fir Tree Inn can be found by the railway crossing close to the canal. Run by Martyn and Tracy Perrins, it is a popular inn and one that hides a sinister past linked to the murders at Ottingley. Just months after murdering Hemming, Thomas Clewes became the landlord of the inn and the public bar is known locally as the murderers' bar.

ETTINGHAM PARK, WORCESTERSHIRE

This brooding and stunning Gothic building sits proud in forty acres of parkland, a favorite location of filmmakers. It was used in the 1963 original *The Haunting*, directed by Robert Wise and based on the book by Shirley Jackson, *The Haunting of Hill House*. Ettingham Park Hotel was even named by the AA as the most haunted hotel in the country!

Ettingham Park Hotel is home to a number of ghosts, and the two related to the waterways are, sadly, those of two children. They have been seen playing in the park near the house and along the banks of the River Stour. Their graves lie in the now redundant churchyard close to the tower. Ettingham Park Hotel certainly has all the hallmarks of a real haunted house.

LAPWORTH

During the winter freeze of January 2002, a strange thing happened along the arm of the Kingswood Junction at Lapworth in the West Midlands. The owner of a narrow-boat had been working on it late and decided to stay the night on board. He had been reading the newspaper and listening to the radio, and at around ten o'clock that evening, with the blackness of the night surrounding his boat, he heard a crack running along it, as if the ice had moved and split. A few seconds later he heard a muffled thud. He raised the alarm when he heard a man thrashing about in the water, shouting for help.

Rushing outside with a powerful torch, he pointed the beam at the spot from which the noise was coming – but the ice was frozen solid. Unable to get close from the offside of the bank, he ran over the small bridge that links the Grand Union Canal towpath to the other side of the cut, taking with him his boat hook. He hit the solid ice, hoping to breach the surface and rescue the drowning man, but strangely the screams gradually ebbed away. Noticing another boat along the bank that had a light on, he went to ask if they had heard anything. 'Nothing,' they said, 'but we sometimes get children down here banging the boats.'

Footbridge at Kingswood Junction.

Barrel vaulted cottage, Lapworth.

The following morning, as he went to the car park of the British Waterways' office at Lapworth, he met one of the lads who worked the bank and told him of his previous night's experience. 'Oh him,' he replied, 'he was drowned when he fell off the bridge one night when the ice was thick on the canal and the towpath too slippery. He'd been drinking at the local inn. You'll never see him, but many a person has told me or one of the other lads about his ghost.'

At the recently closed British Waterways' office at Lapworth on the Kingswood Junction, there was often talk of an old woman who walked around the top room of the building. Even the cleaners heard the footsteps, yet on inspection the room was always empty. On one occasion, the door to the computer server room opened and slammed shut in the middle of a meeting. No one could explain why.

Kingswood
Junction.

Lapworth
Junction.

SALTISFORD ARM, GRAND UNION CANAL

On the Grand Union Canal at Warwick is an old canal workers' cottage haunted by the ghost of an old woman who is dedicated to making life eventful for anyone living there. For years it lay empty because no one would stay there for any length of time. Having lived there just short of a month, one young family fled in the night following hours of objects being thrown around, lights switching on and off and taps turning on for no reason.

The day had started like any other day for the family. Dad was on night shift, so was in bed as the children went off to school and mum to her job in the town. At midday, the father woke up to see an old woman standing at the end of the bed with a vase in her hand, which she dropped as he got up.

She then turned and left the room. He followed, but found no one in the cottage and all the doors and windows locked.

When the children returned from school they noticed a funny smell in the kitchen, like old coal being burnt. As they watched television, a shadow walked across the screen and it switched off. No matter how they tried, it would not turn back on. Into the night, the lights started to dim and blaze to such intensity that it became hard to look at the bulbs. After they were tucked into bed for the night, the old woman appeared in the children's bedrooms and screamed at them to leave before pushing the beds over.

Doors started to bang, taps gushed forth water yet were turned off and the horror that ensued led to mum and her two terrified children running away from the cottage. The ghost still haunts the cottage to this day, though the family do not go out of their way to tell others this.

River Avon, Stratford-upon-Avon

A number of ghosts haunt the theatre here, one being the original owner who died there. Others include an actor who stands to the side of the stage, directing plays or just observing fellow actors. On the Stratford Canal, a ghostly narrow-boat glides silently under the bridge and into the canal basin where it moors up, surrounded by a strange blue-grey glow. If you venture into the town itself there are many ghosts to find, and no better way to do it than with the Falstaff's Experience team, who lead tours around the town and through their own museum.

Stockton Flight

Between Napton and Long Itchington of the Grand Union Canal is the Stockton flight of locks, haunted by the ghost of a boatman, windlass in hand, who shouts to approaching boat crews that the 'boat's coming.' This term is used to tell the approaching boat crew that the lock is set in favour of a boat coming from the other direction, and that they must wait their turn. As the boat is moored up, ready to take its turn in the lock, the man vanishes and no boat arrives.

HATTON LOCKS, GRAND UNION CANAL

Hatton is well known for its challenging flight of locks, known locally as the stairway to heaven. Not for the faint-hearted, this flight of twenty-one locks takes a lot of hard work to get through in one day. Before the remodelling of the current flight to double-width locks, work was hard and the strain of the locks would often take its toll on the boaters. Many suffered heart attacks as they approached the top of the flight. Perhaps it is one such boater who is seen walking along the towpath from the top lock towards the Shrewley Tunnel, before clutching at his chest and vanishing? Is he also the ghost who has been seen sitting in the corner of the old stable building, now a café?

Further down the Hatton Flight is the British Waterways' regional office and training centre, where another haunting has been reported. From the public car park can be seen what looks like a railway signal box, in which the spectre of a bald-headed man is spotted peering out of the windows at passing boats. Some of the pleasure cruisers going through there have spoken of feeling uneasy, and those who have actually seen the ghost say that he is checking up on their boating skills. The upper floor of the box is

Hatton Flight.

seldom used by British Waterways, and some staff members who have seen the man peering out of the windows have gone up to investigate, fearing he is an intruder, only to find the room empty.

A couple once going through the Hatton Flight as the evening light was fading reached the middle lock to find it free. Alf, the owner, was steering the narrow-boat into the lock when suddenly the gates slammed shut and the paddles were opened with such speed that the narrow-boat started to take on water. Sue, his partner, rushed forward with her windlass to stop whoever was opening the paddles in order to slow the rush down. There was no one around, but suddenly a huge white horse appeared, galloping towards her. She jumped out of its way and watched as it continued down the towpath, before merging into the dark. As she looked back up the canal she saw a young woman carrying a wicker basket running after the horse shouting, 'Alfie, don't leave me, it is your child!' as she too vanished into the night.

As Sue looked back at the lock, she noted that the water had calmed down and the lock keeper was standing on the other side of the lock wall looking on. He crossed the gates and told them to be quiet as they passed through Asylum Lock because, 'Eleanor don't like disturbance. She were laundress at the County Lunatic Asylum. Put there 'cos she got in trouble by one of the canalmen. They'd meet up 'ere. Turned out he was already wed. Broke 'er 'eart it did. She comes back whenever she 'ears 'is name – Alfie.' The lock keeper waved them off and they continued to the mooring at the top of the flight.

Mooring up they met another couple from a narrow-boat further up. Recounting their story, the other couple went white. They explained that there had not been a lock keeper there for years and that a keeper had thrown himself into the middle lock in 1860 after his daughter died in childbirth at the asylum. Sue and Alfie had a stiff drink that night, safely locked up on their narrow-boat!

MOATED MANOR, BADDESLEY CLINTON

Baddesley Clinton is a fairy-tale moated manor house, haunted by a monk who rises from the moat where his body was thrown and drifts towards the library where the then owner of the house, Nicolas Brome, murdered him.

Shrewley Tunnel.

As he was well connected, Nicolas was not condemned to death but instead was ordered to rebuild the nearby St Michael's Church that had fallen into ruin during his ownership of the estate. Soon after he had rebuilt the church he was struck down with a fever, passing away in his bed. Because of his crime, he was buried standing upright beneath the threshold of the church. A bloodstain remains on the library floor and a scuffle, scream and footsteps have been heard there faintly in the night.

Shrewley Tunnel, Grand Union Canal

Shrewley Tunnel has one route for boats and a shorter one for the horses to pass up and over the nearby hill. The horse tunnel is frequently used by walkers, in which many have encountered the ghost of a horse that comes charging down the tunnel. As they brace themselves for the impact, it vanishes as quickly as it appears. Others have experienced a feeling of being watched by something that makes them feel uneasy, but nothing has ever been seen. Shrewley Tunnel has some wonderful patterns created by the constant dripping of mineral-bearing water seeping through the brickwork, making a strangely eerie sight.

TWYCROSS, BILSTONE

To the side of the A444, on the road to Bilstone from Twycross, is a gibbet post hanging from which the body of John Massey was placed in an iron gibbet after being executed for the murder of his wife and the attempted murder of his daughter in 1800.

Massey was a wrestler known for his quick temper. When his wife announced she was leaving him he lifted her in the air and tossed her into the mill race off the River Sence. With her heavy clothing and bags she quickly sank to her death. His daughter looked on helplessly, before she too was picked up and thrown in to the mill race. She survived the attempted murder, but passed away from pneumonia soon after her father's execution.

At the mill, the grim spectre of the mother, bags still in hand, appears looking over the mill race where she lost her life. At the gibbet, the daughter is said to look up to where her father would have rotted away before she is joined by her mother, who walks out of the river.

BRAUNSTON TUNNEL

An experienced boat owner had moored up his boat, *Bramble*, on the south end of the Braunston Tunnel, stopping to enjoy a bacon sandwich. It was early in the morning and there were no other boats about on the canal, as he ate his breakfast with his wife sat on the stern. Anxious to get under way before the morning rush of holiday boats began, he sailed into the tunnel. Halfway through he noticed a working boat ahead of him. Thinking the boat must have pulled up in the tunnel for a while he followed on behind, but called his wife on deck to have a look. They both watched as the boat reached the end of the tunnel, before the sunlight streamed in, causing them both to briefly look away. As they exited the tunnel they were astonished to find that the boat had vanished.

Travelling on to Braunston Locks, they thought they might catch up with the boat and share its locks down the flight. Reaching the flight, the man found the locks set in his favor with no sign of the working boat. Part way through the locks he met up with another couple heading towards the tunnel, who confirmed that they had not seen another boat since sunrise, and especially not a working one!

Was it the sun playing tricks on the waters and tunnel walls, or an old-timer taking his last load to store?

RIVER NENE, THE TALBOT HOTEL, OUNDLE

This Elizabethan hotel houses the stairs of the once great Fotheringhay Castle that stood a few miles up the river, where the ghost of Mary, Queen of Scots, appears along the river bank and up at the castle mound. At the hotel, Mary walks down the stairs, as she would have done when she went to her execution. The ghost of an old woman wanders the courtyard out towards the main street. Nearby, at the museum, the ghost of a man is often seen standing in the corner looking at the exhibitions before turning and walking through a blocked door.

YELVERTOFT, GRAND UNION CANAL

Near Yelvertoft, on the Grand Union Canal, the remains of an old timber working boat named *Thelma* once rested. One evening, a group of local youths made a visit to her with a bottle of cider. In their alcohol-fuelled gusto, they decided to try and set the old boat alight and so broke in. Inside, they tried to light the framework with matches, but every time they tried the match was mysteriously blown out. One of the lads had a lighter and flicked on the flame. No sooner had he done so, then an invisible hand grasped his wrist with such force that he dropped the lighter and winced in pain as the grip tightened. He fought against the hand to no avail. At the same time another member of the group took a swig of the cider, and was duly terrified when the bottle was dashed from his hands. The bottle crashed to the floor, cider pouring out across the boat. The frightened lads ran from the boat, leaving behind the one grappling with the unseen force that held his wrist. It was only when he apologised to whatever was gripping his hand that it relinquished its hold, and he ran from the boat to join his friends. After that an old man was seen on the deck of *Thelma*.

Stoke Bruerne.

STOKE BRUERNE

On the upper floor of the waterways museum resides the smoky figure of an old man who tends some of the machinery on display in the room. Perhaps he tended the items in real life and now returns as a ghost engineer?

Out on the canal there is also the spectre of a lock keeper who stands on the side of the locks with a pipe of strong smelling tobacco, watching the crews of the many boats that pass by. The aroma of his tobacco is often reported, particularly on early summer days.

BLISWORTH TUNNEL

Blisworth Tunnel is one of the spookiest tunnels of the British waterways system and has a tragic history of deaths inside the tunnel. During its construction between 1793 and 1805, fourteen navvies lost their lives when the section they were working on suddenly collapsed. Once the bodies that could be removed had been taken out for burial, the rest were left in the collapsed section and the tunnel line changed to the line that it is today.

Some time ago, a couple new to narrow-boating checked the map and set off into the tunnel from Stoke Bruerne. They travelled for some time, emerging at the other end a little confused. They had been three-quarters of the way through the tunnel when they spotted a fork ahead. They heard voices and saw candlelight coming from the left-hand tunnel, so decided instead to go right. As they emerged, they drew up alongside a man from British Waterways and asked about the fork in the tunnel. They were not expecting his reply. He told them of the tragedy that had claimed the fourteen lives, and of the entrance to that part of the tunnel that had been blocked up with some of the bodies remaining inside. The couple had marked the estimated location of the ghostly tunnel on their Nicholson *Guide to the Waterways*, and upon investigating the map found that it was within inches of the sealed entrance.

Another ghostly apparition in the tunnel is that of an old steam tug that is seen powering towards boats, before vanishing. The story goes back to the introduction of steam tugs in order to speed traffic through the tunnel. In 1861 a

Blisworth Tunnel.

master and boy were at the helm of a line of two butties, pulling them towards Stoke Bruerne. They were late emerging, but when they did they were both found to be dead, suffocated by the fumes from the coal-fired boiler. As a result of this sad story, ventilation was introduced in all long tunnels.

The final ghost in the Blisworth Tunnel area is that of Fly Charlie, who pushes lock gates shut so that boats cannot get out. He was a man who spent his life on the canals, and he continues to haunt them in death.

RIVER WENSUM, LYNG

To help the sanitation of St Edmunds Chapel, a river channel was dug from the River Wensum in a loop underneath the chapel and back into the river's main course. Long after the chapel had been abandoned, two fishermen in a boat spotted a silver chalice in the channel. One grabbed it as the other, who claimed to have seen it first, struggled to get hold of the prize too. As they struggled in the boat one of them swore at the other, at which point the chalice rose above the quarrelling pair and fell back into the river, lost forever, as no matter how long they looked they could not find it.

RIVER YARE, BURGH CASTLE

The castle at Burgh is a Roman fort allegedly haunted by a legion of Roman foot soldiers who march out of the main gates towards Great Yarmouth. Inside the fort, a number of visitors have reported seeing a Roman soldier walking across the grass towards the rear of the fort, where he stands on guard for a minute or two before turning and walking into a mist.

RANWORTH BROAD

Deep under the broad is a secret chapel where the monks of the nearby abbey would hide when robbers were marauding, killing and stealing. After a great fire at Abbey Farm, a tunnel was discovered in the cellar that led towards the broad. Such was the height and darkness within, the tunnel was blocked up and the cellar filled in for fear that the Devil may lurk there. Should you be on, or near, the broad on a warm summer evening, you may hear the chanting of the phantom ghosts in their chapel deep below.

RIVER ANT, DILHAM

Not far from the river is the deep water-filled pit known as Seagar-ma-hole, on the site of a church that was sucked down into the pit along with local people and some oxen. Some weeks before, the rector of the parish had warned the congregation that they would all go to hell if they continued to use the church to hide smuggled goods. He gave them a week to remove the items, warning that he would go to the customs and excise men in Great Yarmouth if not. The following day, the rector was recovered from the river where it enters Barton Broad, his throat having been cut.

The story goes that on the day the church fell into the pit, many of the locals had been having a party inside to celebrate the demise of the rector when they heard his voice cursing them to hell for defiling the place of God. The ground began to shake as the whole church, the locals, a wagon loaded with brandy and four oxen were all sucked down to hell. Since then, on a cool winter's eve, the sounds of distant bells ringing and low moans of the wicked people have been heard. Along the river bank, the tall thin figure of the rector walks, wringing his hands for all his worth.

DISS MERE

The mere, which covers six acres, is said to be bottomless and to have a giant fish which lives in a cave halfway down, waiting to catch any unfortunate person who falls in and drowns. Once a year, the fish is said to blow wind, the cause of the annual stink rising from the water. In the winter the mere freezes over and, despite the efforts of the town's officials, people are drawn to the frozen mere where, sadly, someone often falls through the ice and drowns. The body sometimes does not resurface for weeks – if at all.

MERMAID'S POND, RENDLESHAM

For many years, there was a pond in the shape of an S, which formed part of a heath, in which a mermaid lived. However, this mermaid was not a happy one, for a smooth-talking showman who saw her as a source of potential income had tricked her into the pool. For months she put up with being his prize attraction, until a boy threw a stone at her, cutting her head. She roared like a lion, and grabbed the boy and the showman before dragging them deep down into the pond. After a time the pond silted up, leaving the mermaid stuck at the bottom. She returns to lure men to a murky grave, so beware if a beautiful young woman makes advances to you in what is now a forest. The forest is also a place said to be visited by UFOs – just look up information on Rendlesham UFOs for more details.

Mermaid's Pond, Rendlesham.

WALSTAN'S SPRING

Walstan was born in 975 AD to the mystical King Benedict and Queen Blida, and received a calling from an angel to leave home and work hard for a farmer in Taverham. At twelve years old Walstan left home, working so hard each day that he often fell asleep standing upright. He performed a number of miracles for the sick, and was said to be able to walk through a bush of brambles without getting cut. The farmer was so pleased with his work that he wanted to make him the heir to his farm, but Walstan only wanted to borrow two oxen and a cart when the angel told him it was time to leave. After years of working hard for the farmer and curing the sick, the angel told him it was time for him to meet his maker. His strength began to fail as he was placed on the cart and the oxen were let go to wander where the angel took them. When Walstan died, a white dove flew out of his mouth followed by a spring gushing out of the ground, where a well had to be built to hold the water. Those who took the water claimed cures for all sorts of ailments, from the plague to a simple cough.

HELL'S HOLE, TUNSTALL, NORFOLK

The story goes that after a massive fire at St Peter and St Paul's Church, all that remained was the tower, the chancel and the bells. An argument broke out between the parson and a churchwarden over who should take possession of the bells for safekeeping. As they argued, the Devil jumped into the burnt-out remains and grabbed the bells, before leaping off across the marshes whereupon he dug a deep wide hole and diverted the River Bure to fill it. As the rector and the churchwarden rushed to save the bells, the Devil calmly picked up each one and dropped it into the water, clanging as they dropped through the deep water. To this day, the bells can be heard and bubbles rise to the surface, the result of the bells falling to hell.

DEVIL'S AND FRENCHMAN'S HOLE, THETFORD

In the north of the moat, around the castle ramparts located there, is an area known as the Devil's Hole, where a person can summon up the Devil by walking, anti-clockwise, seven times around the area at midnight. Once summoned he will give you one wish, the price being your soul, and that, on a given day, you must summon him once more and follow him to hell.

The Frenchman's Hole on Carr Common is where a Frenchman once ended his life. He had asked a local woman's father for her hand in marriage, being deeply in love with her. The request was refused and he was left in no doubt that there would never be a marriage between them. The Frenchman then arranged to meet his lover so that they could elope together. He waited for days, and as he gazed across the common he saw a figure approach him. A maid had been sent by his lover's father to tell the Frenchman to go home as his daughter had been sent away. Broken-hearted, the Frenchman drew a dagger from his pocket, plunging it deep into his heart before collapsing into the dark waters of the pool. Since then, the lone figure of a man in a long coat stands at the water's edge whilst gazing into the distance.

THURLTON, NORFOLK

Thurlton, Norfolk, is an area renowned for the eerie spectacle of the will-o'-the-wisp or the jack-o'-lanterns. These are caused by the release of methane gas that self-ignites, sometimes creating tall blue flames. Many a visitor or resident in the area has fallen for the misleading lights and perished in the cold waters of the nearby dykes. One such victim was Joseph Bexfield, a wherryman who knew of the ghostly lights, but even so, on 11 August 1809 he must have followed them, thinking they were people crossing the fields. His body was discovered in a dyke with reed roots around it. He is buried in the nearby church, and on the anniversary of his death screams are said to be heard across the dykes.

HICKLING BROAD

During frosty February nights the ghostly beating of a lone drummer is heard floating over the lonely broads at Hickling. In the eighteenth century, a young man had just won the place of drummer boy for his local regiment – a great honour then, as it still is now. He proudly dressed in full uniform and travelled some miles on foot to see his sweetheart. At last he was close, and the only thing that stood between them was Hickling Broad. It was frozen solid and so he decided to walk across the ice, drumming as he walked. Maybe his drumming caused the ice to crack, or perhaps he was just unlucky, but he was never seen alive again. His senior officer thought he had deserted, as he was due to go to India two days after he had disappeared. It was only when a local poacher found the drum floating on Hickling Broad when the ice melted that a search took place. The body of the young drummer boy was found in a strange state of preservation, a broad smile upon his face. If you are lucky enough, you may catch a glimpse of him as he 'floats' across the broad playing his drum.

POTTER HEIGHAM, RIVER THURNE, NORFOLK

Over the River Thurne is the famous three-arched bridge at Potter Heigham, which hosts a powerful image of a ghostly event seen by many local people as well as those enjoying the Broads.

On 31 May 1742, Sir Godfrey Haslitt married the local beauty, Lady Evelyn Carew, in Norwich Cathedral who, it is said, planned the whole event with the Devil for the price of her soul. Little did she realise that the Devil would claim his prize so early, for at the stroke of twelve midnight the poor woman was snatched from the arms of her lover by four figures dressed in black cloaks with white skulls visible from beneath their hoods. Kicking and screaming she was taken to a black coach with four jet-black horses waiting impatiently. Once the victim was inside, the coach tore off down the track towards the bridge, sparks flying from its wheels and the

Bridge at Potter Heigham.

whole thing taking on a phosphorescent glow. Such was the speed it was travelling that, in the centre of the bridge, the coach swung into the stonework, shattering it and causing the coach, horses and carriage occupants to smash through another wall into the fast-flowing River Thurne below.

If you are on a boat or walking home along the river on 31 May, look out for the phantom coach and four cloaked figures as it thunders towards the bridge.

BARTON BROAD, NORFOLK BROADS

As this area was being drained, great tracts of land were taken over by local people who wished to join the upper classes via the medium of ownership. There developed great estates from this new land distribution. A terrible man who ruled his household with a rod of steel took over one of these great areas. When one of his daughters tried to run off with her true love, he followed in pursuit. The eloping pair were sailing off in a rowboat, heading across Barton Broad, when the boat was hit broadside with a large amount of shot from a punt-gun. His daughter was killed outright, and her lover badly wounded. The boat was hauled ashore and the lover told to leave – which he did, fearing he would be the next to be shot. Her father was filled with remorse when he realised he had killed his child. He made a vow to change his ways and begged the forgiveness of his dead daughter. It is said if you are visiting the Barton Broad and you see her smiling face in the water, it should be taken as a sign of good luck.

RIVER BURE, NORFOLK

The ghost of Richard Slater, who worked at the vicarage in Belaugh, haunts the River Bure there in Norfolk. Employed for his handiwork, he had been stealing from houses in the area. As he amassed his stolen fortune he found a good place to bury it, in the grounds of the vicarage. On the night he had planned to make his escape to begin a new life, he was caught digging up the bags of treasures in the garden by the vicar. The vicar challenged him with a flintlock pistol. Slater made a run for it, with all the stolen treasure stored in his pockets and in various leather bags.

Running across the fields he found himself cornered, with the only way out across the river. He jumped in but failed to emerge from the river, and a now large search party had gathered on both sides of the river bank. As they waited one man spotted one of the leather bags, slightly submerged, floating down the river. Inside were many of the pieces of jewellery and coins that Slater had stolen. They even found a silver chalice from the church. After watching the river till daybreak, it was decided that someone should enter the water where Slater was last seen. About 2ft under the river's surface, the upright body of Slater was found, weighed down by the stolen gold and silver. All but three of the stolen pieces were found and returned to their owners. Slater's ghost has been seen running towards the river, before leaping into the middle of it and disappearing.

Not far away the ghost of a woman dressed in a white wedding dress has been spotted along the river bank. Is she waiting for Slater, who never made their rendezvous, having died of a broken heart? She appears on 24 August, just one week after Slater died, so if you are brave enough to have a look do have a walk along the river bank on that date.

RIVER YARE, NORFOLK

Sailing towards Brundall on the River Yare, on 24 June and 18 September every year, is the barge of the Bishop of Brundall, rowed upriver by twenty-eight ghostly figures. The Bishop of Brundall's ethereal barge is dressed in fine silks and cloth, the bishop waving at the onlookers as he passes by before the boat simply vanishes in a cloud of river mist.

RIVER WAVENEY

Once a year, passing by Burgh St Peter on the River Waveney, you ight glimpse the ghostly ship of a North Sea pirate who used the Norfolk Broads to hide from the authorities. He regularly made raids on passing ships and picked up contraband from those hailing from Holland. The headless captain has been seen at the helm of his boat, somehow shouting orders. It is believed that if you can find the last resting place of his boat, you will find his great wealth of gold.

FERRY INN, HONING, NORFOLK

During the Dark Ages a large number of monks dispossessed of their property in France and looking to set up new monasteries travelled to this area. Unfortunately, not all the monks were law abiding, believing that God would forgive their sins. One of their unfortunate victims was a serving wench who was raped by the monks before being strangled, her broken body thrown into the river that passes the Ferry Inn. In the bar and along the river bank the thin woman has been seen in a long green dress, walking towards the coast.

RIVERS BURE AND THURNE

At the confluence of the Rivers Bure and Thurne is Ludham, haunted by a monk who gave away the location of St Benet's Monastery to the Normans. Once he gave up the location, he was beheaded and his head thrown into the river. His figure is seen searching for his missing appendage along the river bank, to fill the black void under his hood. His betrayal led to the abbot and monks being murdered before the monastery was looted and burnt to the ground.

River Waveney, Geldeston Lock

steel

For many years a lady ran the local inn with a rod of steal and she is still reputedly seen in the area. One man, who was camping in the field next to the inn, woke in the night in need of relief and headed off towards the bushes. As he carried out his business, he was embarrassed to see an old woman approaching, crossing the lock bridge carrying a candle in a jar, and followed by a large goose. He watched the odd pair walk towards the inn and enter it. The next day he asked the landlord of the inn who they were. Very casually, the landlord told him, 'that's the ghost of Susan, the previous landlady, and her goose named Grumpy.'

Bishops Bridge, River Wensum, Norwich

The walk that leads to Bishops Bridge, Bishopsgate, in Norwich is the haunt of an old lady with a fatal curse placed upon her. A man saw a little old woman bent double as she struggled to carry a large bag of wood.

Bishops Bridge, Norwich.

He took the wood from her and carried it to the Red Lion, near Bishops Bridge, where she took it back and thanked him. Six months later to the day the man was burnt alive in a fire at his home. None of the surrounding furniture was burned and neither was the building. Others have perished in the same way after meeting the old woman, believed to have been a witch who was burnt at the stake.

In the sixteenth century, many women accused of witchcraft were forced to carry large bags of wood down Bishopsgate to the dungeons below the Red Lion, before being made to walk to Lollards' Pit where they were tied to a stake, often naked, and the wood stacked around them. As the pyre was lit, the accused would scream themselves hoarse whilst cursing the watchers as their skin melted and flesh cooked. The charred skeletons were left in the ashes, never to be buried, so their souls would roam the area for eternity.

OLTON BROAD, SUFFOLK, THE BROADS

The figure of the flamboyant author, George Henry Barrow, is seen in the old summer house where he wrote and the cottage where he passed away. Dressed in a long black coat and wide-brimmed hat, his ghost has a sense of both purpose and calm about it.

RIVER WAVENEY, BUNGAY, SUFFOLK

The Homersfield Bridge crosses the River Waveney, and legend has it that under the arch of this bridge a howling demon was forced into a bottle by the prayers of twelve rectors, after which the bottle was secured to the underside of the arch with a large metal strap. Another prayer was said, that as long as the water should flow under the bridge, then the demon would be contained. Some years later the bridge was in need of repair, so a cofferdam was set up to stop the flow of water under the arch. Suddenly there was a loud howl and a black dog appeared on the bridge, growling and snarling at the fleeing workers before it ran off towards Bungay, where Black Shuck has been seen ever since.

WISSETT, SUFFOLK

Cole's Arch is where the ghost of a young woman is reported to sit on the iron railings before vanishing into the moonlit night. Close by is Paradise Cottage, along Lodge Lane, visited by a grey ghost of a woman who passes through the garden, across the road and into the stream before turning back to the road. Nearby Hallelujah Pond is witness to a phantom horse and cart racing down the hill and into the pond amid a clattering of its wheels and neighing of the horse.

BARTON MERE, GREAT BARTON, SUFFOLK

As with any other mere in the country, the depth of water it contained determined the quality and quantity of crops. If the water was high it would be a good crop, if it was low then yields would be also. Barton Mere was used as such a measuring device, also boasting the ghost of a lady in a long white dress who rises from the waters just before someone in the village passes away, as if she were the guardian sent to take them to the light.

GOLDEN POOL, ICKWORTH, SUFFOLK

In the grounds of the eighteenth-century Ickworth House, now owned by the National Trust, is a pool where the abbot of Bury St Edmunds is said to have had his monks throw chests of gold to keep them away from King Henry VIII's men before the dissolution of the monasteries. The abbot kept a guard of monks at the pool in order to stop the theft of the gold. As time moved on the gold was forgotten, until a scholar uncovered a written text detailing the contents of the chests and reference to their location. After some years of fruitless searching, partly due to the building of Ickworth House and redesign of the surrounding landscape, the pool was found and one of the chests pulled from the water. As the workmen began to break the locks there was a sudden downpour and the chest slid back into the pool down the grassy bank. No matter how much they searched, even dragging grappling irons across the deep pool, nothing more was found. In the summer, the pool appears to glow in a golden light. The ghost of a monk is said to stand by the pool and dogs will not approach it.

River Lark, Bury St Edmunds

The abbey of St Edmund dates back to its early foundations in 1020 when Benedictine monks who guarded the body of St Edmund were granted lands by the King. Over the years the abbey prospered, until the riots of 1327 when a number of monks and the abbot lost their lives at the hands of locals fed up with the high taxes that the abbot placed on them. During the riot the head of the abbot was placed on a long pole and put on top of the bridge into the town, now known as Abbot's Bridge. It is on this bridge over the River Lark that people walking down East Gate Street have seen a monk-like figure glowing as if on fire, running through the inner corridor of the bridge, screaming, before vanishing into the road.

Close by is the Great Churchyard of the town, haunted by the ghost of Maude Carew each 24 February at 11.00 p.m. It is alleged that she murdered the Duke of Gloucester in 1446. Maude was a lady of the royal court, who retired to Bury St Edmunds as a nun to escape its excesses. She was loyal to Queen Margaret, who loathed Humphrey, Duke of Gloucester, and regarded him as a political enemy. When she was asked to help her Queen, Maude jumped at the chance. Under the tutoring of Cardinal Beaufort, Maude quickly gained a deep knowledge of poison.

Knowing that he always got up during the night for a drink, Maude entered the Duke's room while he slept and placed a quick-acting poison on his door handle. As she closed the door behind her she felt giddy, then realised she too now had poison on her skin. There was little time before her impending death, so she ran to the man she was in love with – though he was unaware – Brother Bernard. She told him what she had done as she lay dying in his arms. Brother Bernard, believing he could save the Duke, ran to the room only to discover servants surrounding the dying Duke, writhing in agony. As Bernard watched on, the Duke passed away.

Furious, Bernard went back to Maude and cursed her to walk on this night for eternity, mourning her crime. Minutes later Maude too was dead, after pleading with Bernard to forgive her. Ever since, on 24 February at 11.00 p.m., the ghost of Maude Carew glides from St Mary's Church towards the abbey ruins and is seen at the site of the abbey hospital, where her body was taken. The figure of a monk in brown sometimes joins her on her walk – could this be Brother Bernard?

THE MILL, SUDBURY, RIVER STOUR, SUFFOLK

The mill in Sudbury that sits on the Rover Stour is now a hotel, but it has a long history of hauntings that came to national attention in 1971 when a mummified cat was discovered in the roof space during its conversion. The cat was taken away from the building, and within a week of its removal the finances of the project failed and the studio the cat had been taken to suffered a devastating fire – yet the mummified cat survived. The cat was then taken to a farmhouse in Wickham St Paul which also suffered a mysterious fire. Before the cat could be returned to the mill once more, the building suffered more damage when the heavy beam on which the cat had been found split in two.

The mummified cat finally returned home and is now buried in the floor under a glass cover. It was a medieval practice to brick-up live cats in the belief that they were witches' familiars, and would protect their property. To remove them is said to bring bad luck.

WALBERSWICK, RIVER BLYTH

From the landing stage for the ferry at Walberswick, held in the same family for many generations, have been glimpsed the ghost of an old man and a boy who float across the river on full moonlit nights. The two almost reach the landing stage on the Southwold side of the river, before an unnatural fog surrounds them and they appear to vanish. Many a person has drowned in this fast-flowing tidal river, and their souls are said to linger around its banks.

Further up the river, at Blythburgh, in the church can be seen the marks of the Devil who swept into it one winter's eve, looking for new souls. Disappointed at not finding any he struck the side door, leaving long burnt claw marks.

The foundation of the nearby White Hart Inn dates back to the thirteenth century, with later additions, and was, at one point, the courthouse for the area. It is in these rooms that a prior from the nearby priory has been seen in upstairs rooms and heard walking across the floors where dogs and other animals will not enter.

Not far from here, just before the road crosses the river, an older man and a woman in her twenties wearing a long dress, frilled at the hem, with a large hat on and holding a black horse have been seen. One sighting was reported by a lorry driver from Grimsby, who was keeping to the 30mph speed limit when he suddenly saw the couple twenty yards in front of his cab. Braking hard, he was convinced he had killed them, as the lorry came to a halt a full length beyond the point of impact. Getting out he expected to see crushed bodies behind him, but there was no sign of anyone. After some time searching the hedges, with the assistance of other drivers who had stopped to help, he gave up and went on with his journey. The man, girl and horse have been seen at the same spot a number of times, and they are believed to be the ghosts of a local farmer and his niece who went to the fields at noon each day to deliver lunch to their farm labourers. One day they were making their usual journey when the farmer dropped dead beside his horse. The niece was so upset at the death of her beloved uncle that she died herself soon after – of a broken heart.

River Ouse, St Ives

On the banks of the River Ouse, just beyond Holywell, stands the Ferry Boat Inn. The inn is haunted by Juliet Tewslie, who fell in love with a local woodcutter, Tom Zoul, in 1078. Tom was a selfish lover who would romance Juliet when it suited him and then leave her to pine for him for days at a time. All Juliet wanted was to be loved by and married to Tom. Her love remained unrequited, and such was her grief that that she went to the bank of the river wearing a dress that Tom particularly liked and took her own life, hanging herself from a tree beneath which she and her lover had often met.

Juliet was buried in a makeshift grave, Tom marking it with a large stone. As was the custom at the time, she could not be buried in consecrated ground because she had committed suicide. On the anniversary of her death she was said to be seen to rise from the gravestone. Some years later, a local builder purchased the nearby inn to develop it and found he was one piece of stone short for his new floor. He lifted Juliet's gravestone to place over the gap and since then, Juliet has been an active ghostly visitor in the inn. On 17 March each year she rises from the gravestone, looking around the room in anger before making way to her real grave site by the river. On the anniversary of her death, local people attend a 'rising party' to toast Juliet.

On misty evenings, a barge rowed by monks heads towards Ely, carrying an open coffin containing the body of St Withburga. The body is being taken to the cathedral towering high over the flatlands. The remains were removed from their grave at East Dereham under the orders of the abbot at Ely Cathedral, in order that St Withburga's saintly body could be interred in the confines of the cathedral.

River Colne, Red Lion Hotel, Colchester

Within walking distance of the river is a fine Tudor mansion, now a hotel, that dates back to 1465 when it was built for a rich wool merchant. It is believed to be the oldest coaching hotel in East Anglia. The ghost of a young girl, aged seven or eight, has been described skipping through the large banqueting hall with a smile on her face.

In 1633, Alice Mellor, the wife of the then owner, died in suspicious circumstances. So terrifying was her spectre, apparently returning to the scene of her death, that the room was sealed up and blessed by a group of church elders.

Before the hotel was built, a number of wooden structures used by monks from the nearby abbey to sleep on stood on the site. A huge fire engulfed the structures, killing many monks, with one running across the nearby Castle Park in flames before plunging into the river.

River Great Ouse, Huntingdon

The bridge crossing the river is known as Nuns Bridge after the Benedictine nunnery, St Mary's Priory of the thirteenth century, that stood close to where Hinchinbrooke House now stands, incorporating some of the previous buildings. A nun once met a monk under the arch of a bridge that was once located there. They were caught in the act of lovemaking and taken away to their individual cells, bricked in alive to suffer a slow lingering death. On the bridge, the ghost of a tall nun has been seen walking away from the site of the nunnery, in search of her lover perhaps?

Nuns Bridge.

Manningtree, River Stour, Essex

On the bank of the River Stour at Manningtree took place the hanging of four Manningtree witches in 1645, under the watch of Matthew Hopkins, the self-appointed witch-finder general. There were thirty-six women in all, and many were handed long prison sentences despite being convicted of only minor offences.

One woman, Anne West, was given a long sentence due to testimony given by her daughter, Rebecca West, who also supplied damning evidence against the four women who were then executed for witchcraft. They were the one-legged Elizabeth Clarke, Anne Leech, Elizabeth Gooding and Helen Clark. The screams of the four, begging for forgiveness, can be heard echoing across the water.

Hopkins died in Manningtree and his ghost is said to walk over the bridge in the town and along the river.

Pool, Essex.

Manningtree, Essex.

CHAPTER FIVE

WALES

MONTGOMERY CANAL

On the Montgomery Canal at Burgedin is a former lock-keeper's cottage, near the spot where a young couple were murdered by a vengeful father in the twelfth century. The Welsh princess, Eira, was caught running away with

The old lock-keeper's cottage.

her lover by the King and his men. The King was so angry that the couple were bricked up in a cellar separately and shackled in chains. One brick was removed from each of their walls so that they could hear the other perishing in their tomb. A guard was placed at the door with orders to kill anyone who tried to free them – even the Queen – such was the King's anger at their act. The figure of a sorrowful woman has been reported standing in the garden as well as next to the fireplace in the sitting room.

LAKE BALA

The ghosts of Lake Bala are said to be heard on still nights and sometimes seen as sun sets. Legend tells of a town of ill repute that existed in the now flooded valley. Such was its reputation, weak and wicked people would travel for miles to spend time there. Exasperated locals asked a monk for his help in ridding them of the town, but as he entered it the religious man was attacked and mortally wounded, his dying wish being that the wrath of God would put an end to the evil he saw there. His body was then tossed unceremoniously into the river.

Soon after, there was a massive crack of lightning and a tidal wave of water rushed through the valley carrying stones, trees and buildings, killing and crushing all that stood in its way. The wave reached the end of the valley, dumping its cargo to form a natural lake. The bodies of the people were then dragged back into the dark, swirling waters. As silence returned, the monk floated back to the surface and was recovered by locals who built a small shrine to him.

PONTCYSYLLTE AQUEDUCT, LLANGOLLEN CANAL

On moonlit nights, the figure of a woman in a shawl glides along the towpath over the Pontcysyllte Aqueduct towards the tunnel. Entering the tunnel, she has been known to jump onto boats travelling through it before alighting again at the exit.

DIXTON, GWENT, RIVER WYE

One regular visitor to Dixton was a tramp who used to walk between the towns along the River Wye. He would often pick up parcels that were left out for him by the people of the towns, villages and surrounding farms. As he got older the speed at which he could walk naturally slowed, to the point where he was only travelling a few miles a week, thus inevitably having to leave some parcels unopened. During a flash flood of the River Wye the old tramp, who was taking shelter under a bridge at the time, was washed downstream and drowned.

On moonlit nights he may be seen fumbling with a parcel as he walks towards the bridge through a meadow. If you get your timing right you might also see a tall gentleman walking his dog who was another victim of a flash flood that engulfed the water meadows. This flood was so sudden that whole fields of crops and livestock were cleanly washed away and it was said to have looked like a giant had used a broom to sweep the area spotless.

Haunted Bridge, Wales.

RIVER WYE, TINTERN ABBEY

As with many an abbey ruin, a devout monk seems to have taken up residence as the caretaker of this site, appearing to people whom he perhaps feels may not be taking the abbey as seriously as he would like. One group of students were climbing on the walls when they suddenly felt very cold and noticed a hooded figure slowly walking towards them. Needless to say, they left quickly for their coach.

One couple were standing at the place where the font would have been positioned when they saw, kneeling by a column, a monk who stood up before vanishing in front of them.

DEVIL'S BRIDGE, RIVER MYNACH

In the eleventh century, an old woman looked on as her only cow fell down the gorge into the waters of the River Mynach, before clambouring up the other side. No matter what she did, she could not coax the cow back to her side of the gorge. As she called to it, a tall man in a long black cloak appeared at her side. 'What you need is a bridge to reach the other side of the gorge. I will build it for you, as long as I have the soul of the first living thing that crosses the bridge,' he said. The old lady agreed to the request, and went home pondering how one man could build a bridge overnight.

The following day she returned to find a bridge crossing the gorge, her cow still standing at the far side. She was about to cross the bridge when she remembered the stranger's odd request and she quickly pulled a piece of bread out of her pocket and threw it across the bridge. Her dog gave chase to the piece of bread, thus becoming the first soul to cross the bridge. With a roar the Devil revealed himself and shouted, 'you stupid woman, your stinking dog was not supposed to be the first soul to cross the bridge!' At this point he lifted up his hands and vanished in a loud clap of thunder. Beware the Devil as he tries to trick anyone crossing the bridge into giving him their soul.

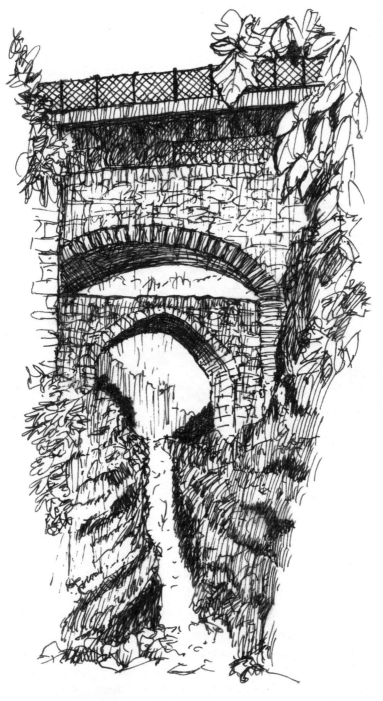

Devil's Bridge.

CRICKHOWELL, RIVER USK

On 21 June every year a large stone on the bank of the river upends itself, dives into the river and goes for a swim. It is believed the stone is a tinker who got on the bad side of a witch when he sold her a tin pot that burnt through on its first use. When she caught up with him about to go for a swim on the river bank, he refused to return her money – so she turned him to stone!

Tinker's stone.

RIVER SEVERN

In years past, when the heads of small kingdoms roamed Europe in search of more land, one king – King Homber of Hungary – was travelling in the north of England with his beautiful companion, Astrilid, when he drowned in the river now called the Humber. Astrilid subsequently found herself at the mercy of some soldiers that had been following her, led by King Locryn. On beholding Astrilid, King Locryn fell deeply in love with her.

He travelled back to Wales with the intention of marrying her, despite his engagement to Gwendolen, the daughter of Corineus, King of Cornwall, who had killed the Cambridgeshire giants Gog and Magog. When Corineus heard the news he was furious, and demanded that Locryn marry his daughter as promised – which Locryn did. He kept secret the fact that, hi real love, Astrilid, lived in a cave below his castle, and that they produced a daughter named Avern.

On the death of her father, Gwendolen was thrown out of the castle and Astrilid put in her place. A year later, the furious Gwendolen returned with an army and smashed down the doors of the castle, killing Locryn and thus leaving Astrilid and her daughter at her mercy. Gwendolen was so angry at Locryn's deception that she had the mother and child bound in chains and thrown into the River Severn to drown. Gwendolen never found happiness, and died a lonely woman.

Should you be walking along the shore of the River Severn, or travelling on a boat up the river, do look out for the two figures dressed in white robes swimming effortlessly upstream towards Bristol. As they pass the place they were thrown in to the river, a woman in green appears to beckon them back. Is this Gwendolen trying to make amends?

River Teifi, Llandysul

Walk along the river bank in Llandysul in the summer months and you may be privileged enough to hear the playing of a harp coming from the river. No one knows who the harpist is, yet the local story tells of a young girl keen to show off her musical skills to the local lord at Cardigan. She was traversing a wooden bridge over the river near Llandysul when it collapsed, throwing her and her beloved harp down into the river below.

Ebbw Vale, Millstream

Once, long ago, the beautiful daughter of a poor man fell in love with the son of a local squire, who seduced her and went through a false marriage in order to have his wicked way with her. She was told to keep the marriage a secret from her father and not to seek out his parents, keeping the secret between themselves. Months later, after discovering that she was pregnant with his child, she heard the startling news that her 'husband' was engaged to another woman. Such was her shame that she hid herself away and had the baby in secret.

With no one left to turn to, she was last seen by her only friend heading to see her father to ask for his forgiveness and hoping to seek revenge on her deceitful lover. What happened later that day is not known, but her body, and that of her son, were found in the millstream having died from a single blow to her head. Her ghost is seen walking along the bank of the millstream, clutching her baby, before crossing in mid-air and turning towards the church where she vanishes.

HOLT, RIVER DEE

In the seventeenth century, two young boys were made orphans when their parents' coach overturned and crashed into a valley, killing all those on board as well as the horses. The only other surviving member of the family was the boys' drunken uncle, their father's brother. He was so pleased to inherit his brother's estate that he quickly forgot he also had the two children to care for, and left them to fend for themselves, eating the scraps of food he threw at them. However, at the the reading of the will some months later he was horrified to learn that his brother had left everything to the boys and just five guineas a year to him.

In an alcohol-fuelled rage, he took the two boys to the bridge over the river and threw them to their deaths in the fast-flowing waters below. One of the brothers survived just long enough to tell a local poacher who had come upon their bodies what his wicked uncle had done, before passing away to join his brother. The next day the uncle was found in a chair at the hall his brother once owned, dead, with a glass of wine in his hand and a look of sheer terror on his face – as if he had seen a ghost, or maybe two?

Two small figures are often seen huddled under the bridge and there sometimes follows the wretched screams of the two falling down towards their watery grave.

CHAPTER SIX

SOUTH EAST ENGLAND

TIDMARSH, BERKSHIRE

On a clear moonlit night in June, the ghost of a young boy rises from the River Pang near the rectory. He is believed to be the son of the rector, and to have fallen in the fast-flowing river whilst fishing with friends who lived nearby. He was swept half a mile downriver where his lifeless body was pulled from the roots of a tree.

REGENCY CANAL

On the Regency Canal in Regents Park there once stood a fine cast-iron bridge, made at Coalbrookdale, with large columns and spans of cast iron on which a brick and stone façade was built. On 10 October 1874, a barge named the *Tilbury* was third in a line of barges being pulled along by a steam tug. The *Tilbury* was carrying sugar, nuts, three barrels of petroleum and five tons of gunpowder when the tug had a flare in the chimney that spread burning embers over the boats following behind. The *Tilbury* was directly under the Macclesfield Bridge when it exploded with such force that the bridge was destroyed, all except for the columns. The barge and nearby boats were also destroyed and the crew of the *Tilbury* killed. The huge explosion caused windows over a mile away to shatter, and great panic ensued until the Horse Guards were sent in to control the crowds and rescue the animals in the zoo.

The bridge was rebuilt in 1876 using the original cast-iron columns with their backs facing the canal so that the rope burns were visible as a silent memorial to the crew. Once a year the phantom line of barges is said to sail up the canal towards the bridge, only to disappear as the shadow of the bridge falls across the barges. One witness reported that they felt a strong gust of wind as the barges reached the bridge and vanished.

BRAMSHOTT, HAMPSHIRE

In 1745, whilst walking along the banks of the stream that runs through the village, Elizabeth Butler suffered a fainting attack and fell into the shallow stream – face down – where she tragically drowned. Her ghost still walks the banks of the stream, one of another fifteen ghostly figures that reputedly haunt the area, including that of the famous actor Boris Karloff who lived here.

ISLINGTON TUNNEL

Islington Tunnel, built between 1812 and 1820, is haunted by a mysterious boggart, who is seen standing on the bow of any boat going through the tunnel after sunset. Local residents are used to the shrieks that come from the tunnel during the winter months, when the ghost is most active.

UXBRIDGE, GRAND UNION CANAL

A small Woolwich butty, *Marcellus*, was found lying on the Grand Union Canal near Uxbridge with a for sale notice tied to her in 1987. Once purchased, the new owner towed her to a mooring in Uxbridge to start her life as a new boat. After she was moored up and as the light faded, an old man was spotted on the stern of the butty, yet on closer inspection no one was found. Over the next three days the figure of the old man was seen several times. The wife of the new owner looked round to see him standing next to her as she steered the butty on tow for a few seconds, and she sensed that he was checking her boating skills.

Once the butty had been converted into a leisure boat, some of the owners' friends were excited at the prospect of spending a weekend on board. They were asleep in the back cabin when a female friend awoke to find the old man entering the cabin from the stern and trying to pull the drop table down. Several times other boats have passed by, later reporting having seen an old man in the cabin or on the stern waving at them before disappearing.

CANAL BRIDGE, CASSIOBURY PARK, WATFORD GRAND UNION CANAL

Travelling along the canal there is a bridge, under which the ghost known as Spring Heeled Jack jumps from foot to foot in his heavy steel jackboots. He has also been known to try and push boaters overboard, so do beware as you travel along this stretch of canal.

OSTRICH INN, SLOUGH, GRAND UNION CANAL,

The inn's origins date back to the twelfth century with a sinister past that is believed to have inspired the penny dreadful story of Sweeny Todd, the barber who gave many of his customers more than a close shave before turning their flesh into meat pies.

In the seventeenth century, the landlord known as Jarman, and his wife, decided to increase their income, having talked to the infamous highway-man Dick Turpin who stayed at the inn between robberies. Whilst not keen on the idea of face-to-face robbery, they came up with a cruel and heinous way of robbing guests at their inn. Jarman would offer the richest guest the best – or blue – room, and before they went to bed would ply them with brandy or rum. Once they were asleep, he would sneak into the room, throw a lever and the poor unsuspecting guest would be dropped into a huge vat of boiling water in which they died. Once the water had cooled, the body was stripped of valuables and any clothing before being dumped into the River Colne. If the traveller had a horse, it would be sold to local gypsies and all knowledge of the victim denied.

This went on for many years until a Thomas Cole, who had been seen entering the inn, was found dead floating in the River Colne a week later. When a visiting magistrate went missing the same week a search party was gathered and the inn searched. The clothing and valuables of not only the magistrate but also Cole and several other victims were discovered in a small room next to the still warm vat, in which the body of the magistrate was found. Jarman and his wife were taken to the gallows and executed for the murder of sixty or more travellers. The ghost of Thomas Cole haunts the upper floors of the inn and the ghost of a woman in Victorian costume has been seen in the room the vat once rested. Do look out for the stuffed Ostrich at the top of the stairs.

BRENTFORD, GRAND UNION CANAL

In 1935, a woman's torso was discovered floating in the canal at Brentford. On the same day, a woman's legs were found in a railway carriage at Waterloo. There was an extensive search undertaken for the rest of the woman's body, but no other parts were found. Many people walking along the towpath in the area have described seeing a tall woman dressed in a white gown coming along the path towards them, before she glides across the canal, wandering up to the railway track.

BOSTON MANOR, HOUNSLOW, RIVER BRENT/GRAND UNION CANAL

Boston Manor was saved by the local community in order to restore the house and gardens that was once the pride of the Clitherow family, from 1670 until 1924, when it was sold to the local authority. For a time it had many uses before being closed to the public and allowed to fall into decay. Happily, things are changing for this wonderful property that once boasted a Cook's garden, based on the plants Captain Cook gave to the owners.

The ghost of Lady Boston is said to run from the manor towards the lake, her throat sliced open, where she disappears. She was believed to have been mur-

dered by her husband and buried in the grounds for having an affair with Lord
Fairfax. Lord Boston told his friends that his wife had decided to go and join
a convent after her affair with Fairfax. Some years later, the body of a woman
bearing a ring engraved with the Boston crest was discovered in the garden.

LONDON CANAL MUSEUM

The London Canal Museum is not only host to a wonderful collection of
artifacts from the golden age of the canals, but also to a lady in a long white
dress and a workman seen walking around the lower floors of
the museum. The building was built in 1862–3 for the famous
ice-cream maker, Carlo Gatti, who had been making do with
older warehouses on the site. It was intended to house the
first of two ice wells in the area. In 1857, Gatti imported
400 tons of natural Norwegian ice that was stored in
the well he had commissioned. During the building
of the second ice well in 1863, measuring 34ft wide
and 40ft deep, a workman, John Parker, fell to his
death after a wooden strut failed.

Since then, staff and visitors to the building
have told of hearing voices coming from the
ice well when it is clearly empty. The well also
emits other strange noises and objects have
been known to move of their own accord.

The white lady has been seen on several
occasions, with visitors thinking she is part of
a re-enactment group there to tell stories of life
on the canals – until she vanishes!

London Canal Museum.

THE GUN INN, DOCKLANDS

The whole area here is crawling with spectres of the bygone era of the
docklands, one property boasting a particularly special ghost. At the Gun
Inn, Admiral Lord Nelson has been seen in the upstairs room, known as

River View, where he often met his lover, Lady Hamilton. Another ghost is that of one of the many smugglers who operated from the inn. The inn has a secret tunnel, with a spy hole, to make sure the revenue men were not in the bar before exiting it. However, they did occasionally catch smugglers at the inn and on the docks, the usual punishment being the death sentence.

HMS *BELFAST*, RIVER THAMES

HMS *Belfast* is one of the most powerful large light cruisers ever built in the world. She served for thirty-two years and took part in both the Second World War and the Korean War, acting in her later life as a peace-keeping vessel. In 1971, she was saved to be preserved for the nation and moored in the shadow of London Bridge. There is one serving member of the crew who never leaves the ship – the ship's cat. He patrols all the decks and is seen on the ship's bridge. Some visitors have felt the cat pass them by, but as they go to stroke him they realise that there is nothing there but thin air.

HENLEY-ON-THAMES

The Bull Inn, close to the River Thames at Henley, has some interesting goings-on, particularly in the bar area. Many of the staff have noticed the distinctive sour smell of tallow candles, while others have seen the faint glow of a candle 'walking' at the back of the bar. In one of the rooms allotted for bed and breakfast trade, a visitor woke to find a cowled figure leaning over him in bed. Needless to say, it caused him to leave very quickly.

Close by is the Kenton Theatre, haunted by a ghost who appears whenever a play about her life and death is performed. *The Hanging Wood*, by Joan Morgan, is based on the life of local girl Mary Blady. She was convicted of poisoning her father and hanged in Oxford for the crime. When the play began production, the cast were surprised to notice a girl sitting at the back of the theatre. Elsewhere, a mirror jumped off the wall and cups were seen to leap from their saucers up to a height of six inches.

OLD LONDON BRIDGE, LONDON, RIVER THAMES

In 1210 a large number of the Jewish population was expelled from the country, with ships collecting them from quays along the River Thames. One small boat collected twelve Jews from the quay just below the Old London Bridge, but quickly sank due to the weight of the luggage on board. All twelve passengers and the two crew perished in the icy flow of the river, their cries for help heard in the winter months, followed by splashing and then a sickening silence.

LAMBETH PALACE, RIVER THAMES

A ghostly barge floats along the river from Lambeth Palace to the Tower of London. On board are a number of crew dressed in grey monks' robes, heads covered, taking Anne Boleyn to her execution, which took place on 19 May 1536. As they approach the Tower, the barge and passengers fade into the walls of the building.

RIVER THAMES

Between Battersea Bridge and Albert Bridge on the river bank at Cheyne Walk, a black bear is often seen rearing up on the bank. This was once a site for bear baiting, and thousands of pounds would change hands every week as bets were placed to see which animal would win the fight against the bear.

At Limehouse the vicar of Radcliffe Cross, who set up a halfway house for sailors who had hit bad times, haunts the area. To fund the charity he would meet rich people arriving off the ships into Limehouse, robbing and killing them. He disposed of their bodies into the river from Narrow Street.

A ghost that screams in agony haunts Cleopatra's Needle before jumping from the top of it, falling into the river below. No splash is heard and no one is seen in the river, yet there are echoes of laughter following the fall.

THAMESMEAD, RIVER THAMES

The leisure boat, SS *Princess Alice*, was rammed in 1878 by a collier class ship in a notorious accident that led to the introduction of rules of the river. The *Bywell Castle* hit the SS *Princess Alice* in the starboard paddle, splitting her in two. She sank and 590 people died, many poisoned by the outflow of sewerage and pollution in the river or from drowning under the weight of their heavy Sunday-best clothing.

Every 3 September, it is said, the ghostly outline of the steam-ship can be seen looming out of a fog, before the river rings out to the shouts and cries of the victims of the accident. Captain Grinstead of the SS *Princess Alice* died in the accident along with many of his family, while Captain Harrison of the *Bywell Castle* went back to sea after the inquest only to disappear in the Bay of Biscay with his ship and crew a few years later in 1883.

SS *Princess Alice.*

BUCKLEBURY, RIVER KENNET

The village of Bucklebury is thought to be the most haunted village in the country, with all kinds of ghosts appearing from the shadows there almost every night of the year. One such ghost haunts the river bed and banks of the River Kennet, which runs close to the village. The monster appears as a large lumbering hulk walking through fences, walls and even parked cars – yet no damage is ever done. It emits a haunting low call as it walks from the village to the river.

Many years before, the area was regularly attacked by a huge monster that did cause a lot of damage. The local population got together and cornered the 'monster', before killing it. Imagine their surprise when they realised it was in fact a mammoth, and not a monster! The beast was buried near the river and the villagers were finally able to enjoy some rest. However, for one week around the anniversary of the death of the mammoth, the creature returns to the edge of the village and the river bed that has since shifted with time. The river bed has eroded so much that, for a while, the mammoth's skeleton was exposed and the blade bone was taken back to the inn by a villager who could identify the remains of the monster. In fact, the landlord of the inn renamed it The Bladebone in honour of the mammoth.

THE BARGE INN, ~~BEDFORD~~ BRADFORD ON AVON, KENNET AND AVON CANAL

The ghost of a boatman has been seen staggering away from the inn, along the towpath, before falling silently into the canal. To dull the pain of the cold on board working boats and the injuries suffered when moving heavy loads, boatmen would often drink themselves into a stupor. Some never made it back to their boat, after tumbling into the canal and drowning.

Some people along the canal have felt that they were being watched, and others have reported becoming breathless, as if they were drowning. Sometimes just the heavy boots and legs of figures have appeared to people travelling along the canal in their narrow-boats – and only when looking up have they noticed there is no body!

Haunch of Venison Inn, Salisbury, River Avon

In this thirteenth-century inn there appears the ghost of a lady in a grey dress who walks its corridors, pausing to look at her reflection in long-gone mirrors. She likes to borrow keys and the guest book, much to the frustration of the staff, who have also experienced cold spots throughout the building.

There is also a mummified hand on display in the House of Lords room, which reputedly belonged to a whist player caught cheating, the punishment being the cutting off of his hand. The demented figure of an old man holding forth the bloody stump is a regular visitor to the inn too.

Chatham Docks

The ghost of Admiral Lord Nelson is often seen pacing the floors and inspecting long-gone rows of flags in the flag loft. When a supervisor died in 1990, his ghost returned to haunt his colleagues. They know it is him due to the habit he had of jabbing people in the ribs if he felt they were slacking, – something which his ghost continues to do.

Chequers Inn, River Beult, Kent

Dating back to the fourteenth century, the inn is a fine example of a smaller public house found close to the river at Smarden, Kent. The ghost of a soldier returning home from the Napoleonic Wars haunts the room in which he lost his life during a robbery. When he booked into the inn he noticed a young maid, who showed a reciprocal interest in him after she spotted the large purse of money he was carrying. They spent the afternoon together, when the maid spiked the soldier's beer with spirits. In his room, before he could make love to her, he fell asleep. The maid began searching the room for the purse, but it took a while for her to find it, so she didn't notice the soldier was waking. He made a grab for his purse, but the maid fatally stabbed him in the heart, leaving him to die alone in the room. When his body was discovered, the maid had already fled with the stolen money. On certain days and nights, the soldier returns to look for his money and the maid, to whom he shouts, 'you will not prosper.'

IGHTHAM MOAT, SEVEN OAKS, KENT

A number of villains were thrown into the moat to their deaths from the fortified manor house walls by a man from a Selby family who once lived in Ightham. The screams of the unfortunate men, who were often tortured beforehand, are heard ringing out across the surrounding lands. Inside, the ghost of Dame Dorothy Selby has been seen; she loved the manor so much she seems reluctant to leave.

CHAPEL POND AND BRICK HOUSE POND, KENT

At Chapel Pond, a woman who lost her unborn child at the hands of her violent husband filled her pockets with stones and walked into the pool of water. Some months later, during a dry spell, her body emerged from the grey depths. She was buried at the crossroads nearby, and since then her ghost has been seen walking from the road into the pond carrying a baby.

Brick House Pond lies close by, where a young man, jilted by his lover, threw himself into the pond to drown. After his body was removed, local people started to talk of a dark shadow following them by the pond and a feeling of menace surrounding them. On quickening their steps suddenly, a white face would appear in front of them, its features contorted in a silent scream.

UPPER LAKE, BATTLE, EAST SUSSEX

Pyke House is a conference centre claiming the ghost of a young woman who haunts its top floor corridor, its back stairs and its grounds. She is dressed in a white nightgown with pale skin and long black hair that flows as if in a breeze. The woman is believed to be the daughter of a past owner of Pyke House, and to have had a brief affair with a local landowner she did not realise was married. She became pregnant, and when she told him what she thought was good news, he blew up in a terrible rage, telling her he never wanted to see her or her bastard child again. Broken-hearted, she returned home in floods of tears before ending her life in the nearby lake that she also haunts, searching in the shallows for something or someone.

ROBERTSBRIDGE, RIVER ROTHER, EAST SUSSEX

The River Rother is normally a gentle river, running through the top of Robertsbridge, yet now and again it rises and floods the nearby fields. On one such day, a local girl called Jane had become tired of being cooped up in the house and decided to go fishing. The best place for this was near Bugshell Mill Farm, where the water was deepest. As the day went on the river rose higher and higher, rushing across the clatters and up to the main village and sweeping away bridges and animals as if they were toys. Jane's parents did not worry about her because they though she was meeting a friend away from the river. Besides, they were needed at home, busy sealing doors and windows against the floods.

The next day the floods were still rising, so Jane's brother Tom was sent up the hill to collect his sister and help carry the family belongings away from the water. Tom had been gone for an hour when the children's mother heard someone banging on the back door, which was already partly under water. What she saw was to stay with her for the rest of her life: her daughter's body had been swept a great distance from the river to her home and was bumping against the back door. The tragic ghost of the girl stands close to the river at Bugshell Mill Farm and passes along the road where her body floated in the flood to her home. She also appears on a bridge in her grey dress, bamboo rod in hand, pointing upriver if there is a flood due to hit Robertsbridge. Should you approach the river when it is flooding, Jane is said to helpfully push you back, away from the raging waters.

CHAPTER SEVEN

SOUTH WEST ENGLAND

EVESHAM, RIVER AVON

As the soldiers of King Henry VIII made their way towards the abbey at Evesham, the silver bells were removed from the bell tower and placed in a boat on the River Avon to be taken to a place of safety. As the monks turned a corner they were attacked by some of the soldiers and the bells were lost to the river. Ever since, on Christmas Eve at the time of the loss, the bells are heard ringing across Evesham and the monks rise from the river and walk towards the site of the abbey.

HEREFORD AND WORCESTER, RIVER WYE

Along the banks of the River Wye appears the figure of a woman with a hunched back and gnarled features who screams out with such pain it is said that, should you hear it, you will feel her discomfort. She is also the bringer of bad news, for soon after she is seen there is said to be loss and grief in the family of the person who observed her. Perhaps she is a friend of the ghost of an old woman who rows a boat up and down the river at Ross-on-Wye, signalling the death of someone in the town?

GOODRICH CASTLE, HEREFORD & WORCESTER CANAL

On 14 June 1646, Goodrich Castle was under siege by Roundheads led by Colonel John Birch, known to be a ruthless soldier. Inside the castle, unbeknown to him, was his niece, Alice, who had sought sanctuary with her Royalist lover, Charles Clifford. Fearing for their lives as the walls were breached, Charles mounted his white charger, pulled Alice up on to the horse, and rode in haste through the back door towards the river crossing. What he did not know was that further up the river there had been a flash flood and, as he reached the river bank, it collapsed, carrying all three to a watery grave in the River Wye. To this day, on the anniversary of the tragedy, screams have been heard coming from the river yet no one is ever seen.

HOARWITHY, RIVER WYE

If you dare to sit on the bridge at Hoarwithy on a winter's evening and watch the River Wye flow below, you may see the ghostly boat of Isobel Chandos who travels the river at night, seeking out souls to add to her crew, sometimes seen trailing in the water behind the boat. Isobel was the daughter of the governor of Hereford Castle under the reign of Edward II. She fell in love with a member of the King's court staying at the castle, and they quickly became lovers. However, their relationship was short-lived as the lover turned out to be using Isobel and her father in a plot to kill the King. When the plot was uncovered her lover was executed and, broken-hearted, Isobel set sail in a boat along the river to the site of the execution where she cursed her former lover.

Whether by accident or design, Isobel was never seen alive again, and her body was found pinned against a fallen tree in the river just outside Hereford. The boat was found broken in two a few yards away. Her ghost is seen travelling up the river towards Hereford, stopping at the site of the execution where she gestures towards the sky before getting back into the boat and rowing into the mist. Many believe that if you see her someone in your family will pass away within a week.

PETTY FRANCE, FEEDER OF THE RIVER AVON

A feeder of the River Avon, Petty France, a house (now a hotel), set in two acres of grounds, is said to have gained its name after it was used to house captured French officers during the Napoleonic War. The house is haunted by one of the previous owners, Robert Banks Jenkinson, recognisable from portraits. He is described as over 6ft tall, tanned, good looking and dressed in a black jacket, sometimes wearing a tall hat. Outside the 'art deco' room the ghost of his mother, Amelia, who died in childbirth, walks towards the main stairs where a young boy sits innocently and then vanishes before the eyes of the bemused guests.

In the attic, an old woman sits in a rocking chair and a sense of sadness surrounds her. Poltergeist activity in the kitchen also causes some upset when knives fly around, crashing into units. There is even a chair that happily takes itself for walks around the sitting room!

NATIONAL WATERWAYS MUSEUM, GLOUCESTER DOCKS

During a family visit to the museum on 29 July 2008, Abigail Williams was taking photographs on her mobile phone to upload to her computer later that day. Little did she know that when she was snapping away at a stack of barrels she would capture an image of a ghostly hand and arm! It was only later when she and her father, Mark, were looking at the pictures on their computer that they saw the arm extending from behind the barrels. The picture amazed staff at the museum, but at the same time it did not surprise them. For years they had heard stories from visitors who had seen a man dressed in a tall black hat and dark clothing. The curator has heard people talking when the museum was closed and other members of staff have seen .and heard people after hours when all the visitors have gone.

The local paranormal investigation society sent Lyn Cinderey, a trusted medium, to see if she could find any rational explanation for the strange sightings in the area. She found nothing except suggestion of a number of orbs around the barrels. These indicate that there is paranormal energy in the spot, but she was unable to make a connection to the ghostly apparition caught on camera.

OWLPEN MANOR, RIVER CAM, GLOUCESTERSHIRE

The property dates back to the 1100s, when it was built for the de Olpenne family who were so upset that their son, Bartholomew, had strayed from his duty as a monk they had him bricked up to die as punishment. He has been spotted walking in the manor and its grounds. He is joined by a lady in grey with a trimmed gown, steeple hat and wimple – possibly Queen Margaret of Anjou who spent her last free day here. On the back stairs, the mischievous child runs up and down the stairs, banging on doors and whistling loudly. In the 1616 wing, the ghost of a wizard who practised witchcraft in the attic haunts it with vengeance, so visitors beware. Children's faces are seen in mirrors, through windows and floating at the end of the beds.

CLEARWELL CAVES IRON MINES, GLOUCESTERSHIRE

These are deep caves formed, in part, by the mining for iron ore over thousand of years, now open to the public on guided tours. There is a great industrial and geological museum there. Some of the ore is also prized as a pigment for artists. In the caves, orbs appear on photographs and visitors report seeing the ghosts of men working in distant corners. The sound of metal banging in far off caves has been heard by staff locking up, and has caused searches to be carried out in the caves in case a visitor was lost.

THE INGLEBURN, THE OLD BELL INN, MALMESBURY

Built next to the abbey and believed to have been a chapel at one time because of eight stone coffins, or sarcophagi, buried under the bar is the Old Bell Inn. Early records show that the inn opened in 1220 as the hostelry to the abbey, before it became an inn for the general public. A number of monks have been glimpsed out the corner of people's eyes, seeming to walk in groups, as if on their way to prayer.

The Grey Lady walks through one of the bedrooms, head down and sobbing to herself. She is believed to be the wife of a monk who died during an attack on the abbey. In another room, glasses rise from the bedside tables and are propelled across the room with such force that they shatter into small pieces.

Next door, a couple returned from the bar to find their door jammed. Staff tried to open it but it remained firmly shut, so one of them climbed a ladder to the window to gain access to the room, which he said felt very cold. A wardrobe had been pushed across the door, thus preventing it from being opened.

Whispers, footsteps and laughter have all been heard in the dead of night by the night porters.

BRIDGWATER, RIVER PARRETT, SOMERSET

Following a leap into the river at Bridgwater, a young man returns to the area of his suicide in order to lure others to their death. He appears to those who may be thinking dark thoughts and seems to feed on their anguish, so much so that he gathers the strength to push them into the waters should the opportunity arise.

At Combwich, on the same river, human sacrifices – usually girls – were once made to the river god so that he would not take the lives of people crossing the river.

On the road that passes through Combwich in a loop is seen a phantom coach and four horses galloping at great speed towards Bridgwater.

MILLSTREAM, RIVER EMS, LUMLEY MILL

In 1630, John Graham, the miller at Lumley Mill, often worked late to keep up with the increasing orders for flour. One night he sensed that he was not alone, and on turning saw the vision of a young woman standing a few feet from him, her face and clothing covered in blood. Not quite believing what he was seeing, and with all the courage he could muster, he asked the woman how she had received her injuries. The ghost told him she was Anne Walker, a relative of his neighbour John Walker. She had been seduced by Walker, resulting in her becoming pregnant, a fact which he naturally wanted to keep quiet as he was married with children. The news had indeed panicked Walker, who was not willing to take on the responsibilities, and arranged for his friend, Mark Sharp from Lancashire, to take Anne far away. Anne thought she was going to stay with an aunt to have the baby before returning to the arms of her lover. However, a short way out of the village Sharp attacked her with a miner's pick and threw her blood-drenched body down an old pit.

The ghost of Anne asked John Graham the miller to reveal the truth about her murder. He was so terrified that he ran from the mill to his wife and stayed in bed for a week. On getting up one day and going to work, the Anne's ghost visited him again. She was angry that he had not told the magistrates about her murder. The terrified miller again retreated home, where he stayed, losing weight and becoming moodier by the day. One day, his self-imposed seclusion became too much for him and he went for a walk in his garden on the eve of St Thomas. Anne appeared to him again, threatening to haunt him until he revealed the truth of her murder.

The next day John Graham went to the magistrate to tell her story. A search was ordered around the area of the pit where, sure enough, Anne's body was found. They also found the pick, shoes and stockings nearby, in the secret hiding place revealed by Anne.

Both Sharp and Walker were arrested for the murder, for which both were executed in 1631. Ever since, the ghost of Anne and a child have been seen in the grounds of the mill, wearing their Sunday best, and in the area locally known as 'Sharp and Walker Gill', Anne's ghost is seen with blood gushing from her head.

CLIFTON GORGE, BRISTOL

The bridge over Clifton Gorge was designed by Brunel, who it is said haunts the bridge and nearby Leigh Wood. It has been the site of many a suicide. One attempt by a Victorian lady in 1864 had an unexpected outcome when she jumped off the bridge, only to find that her skirt ballooned out and acted like a parachute, lowering her gently to the ground. Many a suicide ghost has been seen on the bridge, some even reported to the police who always attend in case it is a real suicide attempt. On summer evenings, the noise of a small aeroplane is heard, engine revving hard before silencing, and the ghost of a pilot appears on the river bank. He is the pilot who crashed into the bridge and then plunged into the river where he died whilst attempting to fly under the bridge.

RIVER FROME, VASSEL PARK, BRISTOL

Vassel Park is a wonderful green space haunted by the Duchess of Beaufort, who loved it in life and seems to have decided to stay. Another ghost is that of a monk, who appears on the bridge across the River Frome where he stands – or rather floats – at the far end of the bridge, before drifting off into the trees nearby.

CHRISTCHURCH, RIVER AVON, DORSET

In 1935, Alma Rattenbury, was arrested and taken to trial for the assisted suicide of her husband. Throughout the trial she kept calm, telling the jury of her love for her husband who had been dying of a long-term condition that would have seen him unable to do anything for himself. She was eventually acquitted, but four days later, on 4 June, she took her own life at a spot known as the Three Arches Bend on the River Avon, just as the railway crosses the river. Such was her anguish that she stabbed herself six times, three in her heart, and fell into the river where she was later found by a dog walker.

She is seen walking the banks of the river, before falling in the cold waters near the bridge and later floating downstream. Those who have seen her tell of the feeling of deep sadness that they experience when observing her figure.

Tarr Steps, River Barle, Exmoor

The prehistoric bridge known as Tarr Steps in Exmoor is said to be the result of a bet made by a giant to the Devil, or Old Nick, that he could not build a bridge overnight. The Devil built the bridge, but then decided it was a good place to lie in the sun so banned anyone from crossing it. It was not until the 1700s that a brave rector walked across the bridge in defiance of the Devil. Not wishing to turn back, he argued with the Devil and won the right for all to cross the bridge except on the one day a week the Devil decided to sunbathe. Since then, tradition decrees that when a shadow is cast over the middle of the bridge you must not cross, as the Devil is relaxing.

Devil on stone bridge.

RIVER EXE, EXETER

The River Exe passes through the county town of Exeter, where a ghostly Viking longship sails along it. Vikings plagued the area for many years, causing great resentment, so when a longship was ambushed on the outskirts of the city and burnt, killing all on board, there was much celebration. Ever since then, the longship with its crew of angry men has been seen upriver as far as the weir.

NEAR NEWTON ABBOT, RIVER BOVEY, DEVON

Close to a footbridge off Summer Lane, near Preston, Devon, has been seen the ghost of a tinker, a small man in a large coat far too big for him with a small hat on the top of his head. The ghost runs away from something apparently following him, before falling into the river and disappearing. He is believed to be a travelling tinker who sold tin pots and items of gold jewellery, for which he was murdered in the 1700s.

AVETON GIFFORD, DEVON

Along the track from the River Avon to the ferry cottage is seen the ghost of a broken-hearted ferryman. As he grew older, the landowner, fearing the old ferryman would fall and drown in the river, blocked up the steep steps down to the river from his cottage. In doing this he cut off the income the ferryman had come to rely on – the large number of people he would row from bank to bank across the river. He died in the 1750s within weeks of the steps being blocked, and is buried in the nearby churchyard.

BRAUNTON BURROWS, RIVER TAW, DEVON

During the summer months the tranquillity of the nature reserve at Braunton Burrows is sometimes shattered by the loud shouting of a ghost commonly known as Old White Hat. He looks like a cavalier with a big white hat and calls out 'ferry' at the top of his voice to a ferryman who never comes. Who he is no one knows, but at least he does not shout too often, or in the winter months.

The beautiful sandy beach around the corner from Old White Hat is the haunted of William de Tracy, condemned to make a rope out of sand in order to escape his curse. Should he get close to finishing the task, a large black dog appears and shoots flames out of its mouth, burning the rope so the poor man has to start all over again. What William de Tracy did is not recorded, but it must have been something really quite terrible.

ROYAL CASTLE HOTEL, RIVER DART, DEVON

Standing proudly on the banks of the River Dart is the old coaching inn, the Royal Castle, home to an unusual haunting. In the courtyard, a fight breaks out with a number of ghostly men dressed in early period naval uniform. They fight in silence, oblivious to their onlookers. In the hotel itself, a gentleman ghost walks the corridors in search of something, mumbling to himself as he toddles along.

KITTY'S STEPS, LYDFORD GORGE, DEVON

In the seventeenth century an old lady, known locally as Kitty, was returning home one summer evening along a short cut that passed a waterfall; she knew the area well from playing there as a child. When she failed to arrive home her family went out looking for her, without success. The next day more people joined the search, yet it was not until the seventh day that her red scarf was found near the waterfall, as well as a wicker basket. Kitty's body was never found, and every year on the anniversary of her death her ghost is said to appear at this spot, looking into the pool.

In 1968 there was another tragedy in the pool when a soldier cut through the gorge, following in Kitty's footsteps, remarkably on the same date. He was missing for several weeks before his body was found below the waterfall. Even the coroner felt that there was something unnatural about the area, and in his summing up at the inquest into the soldier's death said, 'He could have been overcome by the atmosphere of the gorge, which I personally think is not a cheerful place even in daytime'.

Lydford Gorge.

THE FISHERMAN'S COT, RIVER EXE, DEVON

At this riverside inn a young maid has been seen and heard in the bar area, smiling and laughing. She is known to pinch the bottoms of any young men she takes a fancy to. On the bridge near the inn a coach and four horses race towards the town with a headless coachman steering them on.

THE SILENT POOL, CHAMBERCOMBE MANOR, DEVON

This manor's most famous ghost is Kate, who walks its corridors and stands next to the silent pool in its grounds, looking across the garden back to the manor. Her story is one of love and sadness. She was the daughter of William Oatway and a lovely Spanish woman he rescued after his father, a local wrecker, had set a trap for a passing ship. An oil lamp attached to a donkey that was made to walk along the cliff tops led sailors to think it was a safe signal light from shore. Only when they crashed onto the rocks did they realise the trick – too late. Eventually, William married the Spanish woman he had nursed back to health and they became tenants of Chambercombe Manor, a property William had always loved and hoped one day to own.

They spent many happy years there and had a daughter, Kate, to add to their joy. In time, Kate grew up to become a beautiful young woman who turned the head of many a man in Ilfracombe on the occasions that she shopped there with her mother. One such man, Wallace, an Irish captain of a small pirate ship, fell deeply in love with Kate and she with him. They walked the cliffs on the summer evenings to Chambercombe, where they often joined her father and mother for supper.

Some months later they were married in Ilfracombe, setting sail for the high seas before settling in Dublin. Both parents were upset with their daughter for leaving, despite her promise she would return one day. As far as the locals knew, she never did return to her happy home. At least that was the case up until 1865, when a new tenant was repairing the roof after a storm and noticed a blocked-up window that could not be seen from the ground. Inside the manor he realised there was a sealed-up room between Lady Jane Grey's room and the adjacent one. He and his wife broke through into the room to find a large four-poster bed inside with moth-eaten curtains around it.

Slowly pulling the curtain back, by the light of a candle the couple saw a white skeleton beneath a decaying shawl. On the table nearby was a letter on parchment alongside a purse containing some gold coins and jewellery. In the letter was the story we have come to know.

One stormy night William had walked down to the cliffs to see if his father was up to his wrecking tricks and saw that a small schooner had floundered on the rocks. As he looked down on the wreckage, William heard muffled cries from the rocks below. Clambering down the cliff, he discovered the body of a woman whose face was badly smashed by the rocks, so much so that she was unrecognisable. He carried her to the manor and, with the help of his wife, bathed and bandaged her wounds. While they were getting the wet clothes off her, William found a purse containing gold coins and jewellery. There was enough money in the purse to buy the manor, just what William had always wanted to do for his wife and daughter.

For a few hours, the poor woman struggled to breathe due to her broken face, losing her fight to stay alive and passing away in the early hours of the following day. Both William and his wife felt there was something familiar about the woman, but did not know quite what. William removed the treasure and placed it in his desk so he could buy his beloved manor. As he did so, the captain of the custom and excise men knocked on the door of the manor asking if anyone had passed them heading towards the sea. Fearing he would be linked to his father's wrecking practice, he denied seeing anyone pass. As the captain departed he also said they were looking for Kate Wallace, who had been on board the schooner with her husband, but they had yet to find her.

Shocked by the realisation that the dead woman in their living room was their daughter, William broke down in tears as he closed the door to the outside world. Such was their sense of loss and guilt, William and his wife placed their four-poster bed in the room and lay their daughter's body on it, in her mother's best dress and shawl. William wrote the letter detailing the unfortunate story and placed the purse of treasure beside it before sealing up the room, inside and out. William and his wife left the manor, never to be seen alive again.

Kate's ghost is joined by a friendly gentleman who likes to kiss female visitors, a lady in a long dress and two children who skip around the manor.

RIVER WULF, WEST DEVON

The village of Broadwoodwidger could once only be reached by crossing the ford that would often rise suddenly, catching unsuspecting victims and washing them down the river. There is a gigantic, yet kind, spirit at the place, said to pick up people and animals and carry them across the deep waters, putting them down softly.

RIVER TEIGN, SHALDON BRIDGE

The bridge stands on the same line as that of the first wooden bridge that began to collapse after sea worms attacked it and bore through the core of the wood. The later bridge is made of steel and concrete. The ghost of a small boy stands on the rails in his swimming costume before jumping off the bridge. Strangely, in the 1990s it was reported that some children's clothing was found on the bridge and never claimed. At the centre of the bridge stands a tall figure in a top hat who gazes out towards the sea and vanishes as quickly as he appears.

ROWBROOK, RIVER DART

On Dartmoor, as the river makes its way to Dartmouth, a number of large stones stood in the river near Rowbrook, said to be the cause of a death once a year. The stones call the name of their victim on the wind, enticing them to the river's edge, whereupon a white hand appears and forces the victim into the river to drown. For days after, the soaking wet ghost of that victim appears on the largest stone, sobbing away.

River Dart, Devon.

CRASIWELL POOL, DARTMOOR

This is a place that local people will not pass at night, or in the daylight if they can help it, for its dark brooding bottomless waters hold many secrets. The spirit of the pool knows who is going to die during the year, and will tell anyone passing. The sounds of a tormented soul can be heard coming from the pool year round.

Nearby is Cranmere Pool, which lies in a hollow from which the River Okement runs northwards to Oakhampton. The pool is the home to the bad spirit of Benjie Geare, who was five times Mayor of Oakhampton and who died in 1701. He haunted Oakhampton to such an extent that the townspeople paid a vicar to lay the ghost to rest. Using a prayer, the vicar led the ghost up the hill to the pool where he set him the task of bailing out the water with a sieve. Benjie obliged and for many years was kept quiet, but, becoming bored of the work, he waited until a sheep walked by and killed it. He used the sheep's skin to make the sieve into a cup and bailed the water out with such force that the River Okement broke its banks and flooded Oakhampton.

Soon Benjie was back in town, and this time he threw every known trick at the townspeople. Eventually, with the help of a vicar who addressed the ghost in Arabic, the ghost changed form into a black pony that was able to be controlled. A bridle was put on the pony and a young boy was told to take it to the pool, remove the bridle and leave without looking back. The boy got to the pool, removed the bridle and started to walk away, but being young and curious he wanted to know what was happening and turned around to see the pony leaping into the pool. Sadly for the boy, a hoof hit him and he was blinded in one eye. Benjie still haunts the pool as a black pony, or sometimes as a crouching dwarf who capers from side to side in the pool.

DOZMARY POOL, CORNWALL

Like the pool at Childs Ercall in Shropshire, Dozmary Pool has many stories surrounding it as it sits in its lonely spot on Bodmin Moor. The pool is said to be where Sir Bedivere took the sword Excalibur, to throw back to the Lady of the Lake after the fateful battle of Camlan when he and King Arthur were the only survivors. Arthur lay mortally wounded, and charged Bedivere with the return of the sword. The brave knight approached the pool with the exquisite Excalibur, but he is said to have failed in his attempts, and instead returned to the King in the hope that the sword would return England to Arthur. When Arthur lay on his bed with just moments to live, Bedivere returned to the pool and finally threw the sword into the deep waters. As the sword flew across the lake, the hand of a beautiful mermaid reached out from the water and caught it before returning to the depths with Excalibur held high.

BOSCASTLE, RIVER VALENCY

Boscastle's famous coaching inn, the Wellington, survived the great floods of 2004 when the river swept through the village, causing great devastation. It is also significant for housing many ghosts; the owner of the hotel has witnessed one of them. Once, when he was working on reception, he saw a gentleman walk past him wearing a long leather coat, boots and gaiters and a frilled shirt, the garb of an eighteenth-century coachman. As he turned for a moment to answer the telephone he lost sight of the 'guest'. Later on, when he was telling a member of staff about the man in costume, his employee finished off the description – he too had seen the ghost, but his experience involved the man vanishing through a wall.

Another ghost is that of a cloaked figure surrounded in a grey mist that travels across the landing and then up to the tower, where it is seen to drop to the ground. Some years ago, an assistant housekeeper was jilted in love and threw herself to her death from the tower – could this be her ghost? On the ground floor, there is an unusual ghost that dogs seem to like, as they often follow it around the inn. Finally, a dark shadow slides down the stairs and into the cellar on a regular basis, described by many of the staff and guests.

BIBLIOGRAPHY

Brooks, John, *The Good Ghost Guide*
Brown, Theo, *Devon Ghosts*
Dixon, Jeanette, *Welsh Ghosts – Ysbrydion Cymru*
Haining, Peter, *The Dictionary of Ghosts*
Harper, Charles G., *Haunted Houses*
Hole, Christina, *Haunted England*
Hughes, Jean, *Shropshire Folklore, Ghosts and Witchcraft*
McCarthy, Christine, *Some Ghostly Tales of Shropshire*
Marsden, Simon, *The Haunted Realm*
Neal, Toby, *Shropshire Since 1900*
Poole, Keith, *Britain's Haunted Heritage*
Reynolds, Hazel, *Ghosts and Legends of Northumbria*
Sampson, Chas, *Ghosts of the Broads*
Seymore, J. & Neligan, H., *True Irish Ghost Stories*
Spencer, John & Anne, *The Ghost Handbook*
Tegner, Henry, *Ghosts of the North Country*
Underwood, Peter, *A–Z of British Ghosts*
Underwood, Peter, *Gazetteer of Scottish Ghosts*
Underwood, Peter, *Ghosts and Haunted Places*
Underwood, Peter, *Ghosts of Cornwall*

British Waterways/Waterscape website (with permission)

BBC Radio Shropshire
BBC Radio Suffolk
BBC Regional news features
Independent radio stations

ITV News
Towpath Talk
Paranormal magazine
www.paranormaldatabase.co.uk

In addition, I am grateful for the many first-hand reports given to me as part of my venture into the world of the shadows of our waterways.